MATT OLDFIELD
UNBELIEVABLE
FOOTBALL
FIVE-MINUTE
AMAZING TRUE STORIES
ILLUSTRATED BY
OLLIE MANN

# CONTENTS

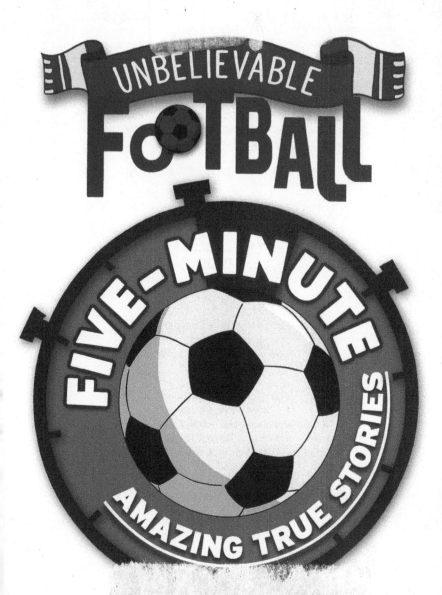

**For Arlo, Ava, Freddie and Jack. The Class of 2021/22.**

First published in Great Britain in 2024 by Wren & Rook

ISBN:  978 1 5263 6701 3

1 3 5 7 9 10 8 6 4 2

Wren & Rook
An imprint of
Hachette Children's Group
Part of Hodder & Stoughton
Carmelite House
50 Victoria Embankment
London EC4Y 0DZ

An Hachette UK Company
www.hachette.co.uk
www.hachettechildrens.co.uk

Printed and bound in Great Britain by Clays Ltd,
Elcograf S.p.A.

# INTRODUCTION

# THE WARM-UP

## Introduction: The Warm-Up

We all know the best way to spend 90 minutes, don't we? Playing a full game of football, *DUH!* Closely followed by . . . WATCHING a full game of football. And then . . . spending 90 minutes READING about football!

So, for our fifth adventure into the world of Unbelievable Football, we've created an all-new match-day experience for you: **eighteen fantastic five-minute stories** (the perfect length for reading at breakfast, bedtime or any time in between) packed full of football action, drama, and all-out entertainment. And of course, all are totally true!

Do I need to do the maths for you? Oh, OK then . . . 18 x 5 = **90 minutes!**

We've even added on six minutes of injury time, in the form of six shorter '**Weird & Wonderful**' stories, and then, as if you won't already have had enough football fun . . . 30 minutes of exciting extra-time tales that end with dun-dun-duuunnn . . . PENALTIES!!

So, other than spot-kicks, what else will you find in this book? Well, a bit of everything, really, as long as it's a) unbelievable but true, and b) involves football.

You'll read stories about all sorts of things, from:

- A one-handed World Cup winner to a magician goalkeeper
- A heroic white horse to the invention of red cards
- Fake injuries to stolen paintings

While these stories are intended to take roughly five minutes to read, some of you might whizz through, some of you might take your time with. Don't rush it, and have fun. Either way, trust me, you're going to enjoy ALL of them, kicking off with:

- The game's most surprising saviours in **'Unlikely Football Heroes'**
- Inspiring drama in **'Incredible Comebacks'**
- Some frankly ridiculous situations in **'Help! New Players Needed'**

Then, after a quick half-time break, we go again with:

- Shocking foul play in **'Red Cards and Dirty Football'**
- The full range of emotions in **'Football Lovers and Haters'**
- The heroic fight for equality in **'A Game for Everyone'**

And to finish things off in style?

- A love letter to the power of football in **'Changing Things for the Better'**
- The nerve-wracking world of **'Last-Minute Match-Winners'**

Phew, after all that football-reading excitement, you're really going to feel as if you've played a full, end-to-end game yourself!

So, what are you waiting for?

**Ready, get comfortable, goooooooo!**

# FIRST HALF!
## KICK-OFF

Warm-up? Done.

Game-plan? Sorted.

Dressing-room dance in front of all your teammates? Only if you're feeling brave!

Right, it's time to get this book STARTED! I hope you're ready because anything can happen in the first 15 minutes . . .

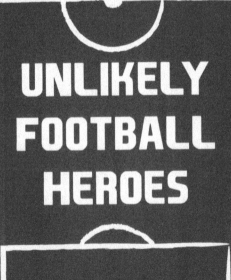

# CHAPTER ONE

## UNLIKELY
## FOOTBALL
## HEROES

They say heroes come in all shapes and sizes, and that's certainly true when it comes to football. Just look at Kingsley, the mascot of Scottish club Partick Thistle, designed by artist David Shrigley in 2015.

The big yellow mascot has the body of a human being and a huge head that looks like a child's drawing of the sun crossed with an angry Lisa Simpson. But despite his slightly scary appearance, he's become so popular that they even made an exhibition about him at the Scottish National Gallery of Modern Art! Don't believe me? Ask an adult to show you on the internet.

Inspired by Kingsley, this section is all about celebrating the game's **most unlikely heroes,** including teams and individuals, players and non-players, humans and, first up, an animal . . .

**Your five minutes start now . . .**

# The Horse Who Saved the FA Cup Final

Here's a fun question for you: if you needed to clear thousands of people off a football pitch as quickly (and safely) as possible, what would you do? Let off a stink bomb? Announce 'Free phone giveaway!' in the streets outside? Get your grandma to sing 'God Save the King'?

Well, on the 28 April 1923, the London Metropolitan Police had to tackle exactly that problem, and their successful solution? To bring on the horses!

It was a day of great excitement in the English capital, especially for football fans – the world's new biggest and greatest sporting arena was about to open!

Soon, the stadium's name would change to 'Wembley', but for now, it was the 'British Empire Exhibition Stadium' (or the 'Empire Stadium' for short), because it had been built for the upcoming British Empire Exhibition of 1924.

In the years after the First World War (1914–18), Britain's position as a world leader was under threat from growing powers such as the USA and Japan. The plan was to show everyone just how strong and united the British Empire still was by holding a huge celebration.

But before that, what better way to open the stylish new national sports ground than by hosting the biggest match in English football – the FA Cup final! Since the cup's launch in 1871, the final had traditionally taken place at stadiums across London. First, the Kennington Oval, then Crystal Palace, and then Chelsea's Stamford Bridge. But from 1923, the FA Cup final would have a beautiful new 'forever home'.

Amazingly, the 'Empire Stadium' took just three hundred days to build (the new Wembley, on the other hand, took more than four years to build, 2003–07!), and the work finished only four days before the big event. Phew, just in time! But in all the rush and excitement, the English Football Association had made a MASSIVE mistake. With space in the new stadium for more than

15

126,000 people, they decided tickets wouldn't be necessary for the FA Cup final. No, instead, they would just let everyone in – the more the merrier!

Really? With the match due to kick off at 3 p.m., the stadium gates opened at 11.30 a.m. and at first, the flow of people was calm and steady. Mostly, they were fans of the two finalists, Bolton Wanderers and West Ham United, but there were also supporters of other London clubs who just wanted to see the new stadium. No problem, everyone was welcome! Apparently . . .

By 1 p.m., however, things were no longer calm and steady. So many people had entered the stadium that at 1.45 p.m., the gates had to be closed. Sadly, that didn't solve the problem. At 2.15 p.m., lots more 'fans' forced their way in, leaping over the turnstiles and causing even more chaos. 'They're storming the stadium!' worried spectators began to shout, as they flowed out on to the pitch to avoid the crush. Instead of 126,000 people, they think the crowd was probably closer to 300,000!

What a dangerous disaster. Would the FA Cup final have to be cancelled? No, they couldn't do that because King George V arrived at 2.45 p.m. and had made his way through the crowds to the royal box. Now, the game had to go on. But how?

First, the footballers gave it a go. At 3.15 p.m., the two teams walked out on to the pitch to ask the people to move back, but instead of listening to their heroes, the supporters all tried to hug them instead. The players were soon trapped, and for poor West Ham forward Jimmy Ruffell, it was a particularly painful experience. He had a shoulder injury, so all the handshakes and back-slaps really didn't help!

OK, player power wasn't working, so it was time for Plan B – Police Constable George Scorey and his dashing white horse.

For Scorey, it all began because he wanted a cup of tea . . . He had been on duty in Westminster since 6 a.m., so he decided to stop at Rochester Row police station for a sit-down and a hot drink. That was the idea, anyway, but when he walked in, a voice quickly called out, 'Scorey, I've got a job for you!'

Minutes later, he was on his way to the Empire Stadium, with the enormous task of trying to clear the pitch of thousands of people.

GULP!

When he arrived at the stadium, things didn't look good. 'I saw nothing but a sea of heads,' he said afterwards. 'I thought, *We can't do it, it's impossible.*'

But despite not really being a football fan, PC Scorey was about to go down in football history. He didn't save the FA Cup final on his own, though. No, he had four very important hooves there to help him. While the policeman sat up high shouting instructions for the fans to link arms and move back step by step, his beautiful police horse did the hard work down below, slowly and safely nudging the supporters off the Wembley pitch in a calm and majestic manner.

'He pushed forward quietly but firmly, and the crowd made way for him,' George Scorey later explained. 'The

horse was very good – easing them back with his nose and tail, until we got a goal line cleared'. Soon, the whole pitch was cleared without any major injuries, and the final was able to kick off – amazingly only 45 minutes late. Hurray!

But, back to the hero of this story. George later said,

'It was mainly due to the horse. Perhaps because he was white, he commanded more attention.'

Come on, George – the heroic horse does have a name, you know! It's 'Billy', and they had been working together for three years, since he was a fresh-faced seven-year-old called 'Horse no. 62' (I'm talking about Billy, not George!). Thanks to his game-saving efforts, he was now a football hero and the most famous horse in Britain.

Although Billy wasn't the only police horse there helping at the Empire Stadium that day, he's the one that everyone remembers. Is that because he was the only white horse? Well, no, Billy was actually grey, but you can't really tell that from the black-and-white photos and videos. Plus, 'The Grey Horse Final' doesn't sound anywhere near as cool as 'The White Horse Final', which is what it became known as.

Now, seeing as this is a football book, we should probably talk about what happened in the actual match. Bolton Wanderers lifted the FA Cup trophy after a 2–0 win, and the two to three hundred thousand spectators certainly played their part.

In the second *minute* of the match, West Ham defender Jack Tresadern went to take a throw-in and got lost in the crowd! By the time he found his way back on to the pitch, Bolton forward David Jack had already fired a shot past the keeper, which then hit a group of West Ham fans who were squashed in right behind the goal. *Nooooooo* and *owwww* at the same time!

Supporters may have been involved in the second goal too. Jack Smith scored it, but according to the furious West Ham players, it was a Bolton fan on the touchline who set him up, rather than a teammate.

All in all, it was a really bad day for West Ham. But even so, there's still no excuse for what their coach, Charlie Paynter, said afterwards: 'It was that white horse thumping its big feet into the pitch that made it hopeless. Our wingers were tumbling all over the place, tripping up in great ruts and holes.'

Hey, no way! Whether you're a West Ham fan or not,

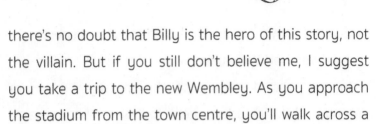

there's no doubt that Billy is the hero of this story, not the villain. But if you still don't believe me, I suggest you take a trip to the new Wembley. As you approach the stadium from the town centre, you'll walk across a footbridge, and what is it called? Yes, that's right – 'The White Horse Bridge'.

So, let's end by giving three 'neighs' for Billy, the horse who saved the 1923 FA Cup final. And don't worry, the FA learned its lesson. After 1923, only the correct number of people were allowed in to watch matches, and stadiums are much safer these days. Phew!

## The Doctor Who Played His Part on the Pitch

So, from a game-saving horse to a life-saving human . . . Our next unlikely football hero wasn't a player out on the field – no, he was just a fan in the stands. Well, to start with, anyway . . .

On Saturday 17 March 2012, Dr Andrew Deaner was sitting with his brothers, Jeremy and Jonathan, at White Hart Lane, watching his favourite football team, Tottenham Hotspur, play against Bolton Wanderers in the FA Cup quarter-finals. And, for most of the first half, he was fully focused on the exciting, end-to-end football action in front of him:

*GOAL!* Tottenham's Gareth Bale scored his first FA Cup goal . . . but at the wrong end. An own goal! Oops!

*GOAL!* Five minutes later, Bale raced up the right end

and set up Kyle Walker to score the equaliser. Hurray!

In the 41st minute, however, with half-time approaching, something else caught Deaner's attention.

*'My vision is going. Everything is blurred. Through the pain I begin to realise I have never had a headache like this before in my life . . . A split second later my head smashes into the White Hart Lane turf.'*

In the middle of the pitch, away from the ball, a player had suddenly collapsed to the ground. It was Fabrice Muamba, Bolton's tall, talented, 23-year-old central midfielder.

Born in the African nation of Zaire (now the Democratic Republic of the Congo), Muamba had moved to England with his family in 1999, when he was eleven. French was his first language, and he didn't know any English at all when he arrived in London, so he let his football skills do the talking instead.

Three years later, he joined the Arsenal academy, where he stayed for five happy years, while also representing each of the England national youth teams, from Under-16s to Under-21s. In 2007, he moved from Arsenal to Birmingham City, and when they were relegated a year later, Bolton signed him for £5 million.

On that life-changing day in 2012, Muamba was still a young player with a bright Premier League future ahead of him, but suddenly, that was all in doubt. As he lay there on the grass, not moving, a group of players gathered around him.

What had happened to him? No one seemed to know, but surely it had to be something very serious for a fit and healthy footballer to fall to the ground like that. A quiet, anxious atmosphere fell over the stadium. But Deaner wasn't going to wait around to find out what the problem was. After all, he wasn't just a football fan, he was also a trained and experienced doctor. Not only that, his job was to help people with heart problems – people like Muamba, perhaps . . .

'I should go down there,' he told his brothers. 'I could help.'

So, when the game stopped and the Bolton team

doctors and physios started doing CPR (full name: 'cardiopulmonary resuscitation', an emergency treatment for people who aren't breathing) on Muamba, Deaner got out of his seat and went down to speak to the stewards.

'Look, I'm a heart specialist,' he explained to them. 'I need to get on the pitch.' Eventually they let him through.

With 35,000 worried fans watching, Deaner sprinted across the pitch, past the other twenty-one devastated footballers, and over to where Muamba lay.

'How can I help?' he asked the Bolton team doctor, Jonathan Tobin.

Under pressure, Deaner didn't panic. He knew exactly what they needed to do next: keep giving high-energy shocks to Muamba's heart in the hope of getting it started again.

*Five, six, seven, eight . . .*

The minutes passed, and Muamba still didn't wake up, but they kept going with the CPR – on the pitch, then in the tunnel, then in the ambulance, and finally at the London Chest Hospital, the place where Deaner worked. Swapping his casual clothes for hospital scrubs, the doctor stayed there every step of the way, doing his best to bring Muamba back to life.

And amazingly, Deaner – together with Tobin and the team of medical staff at the London Chest Hospital – succeeded. The thirteenth shock didn't work, and neither did the fourteenth, but after the fifteenth . . . hurray, there was a heartbeat! The sound was only faint, but it was something. After 78 minutes without breathing, Muamba had come back to life!

'Waking up in hospital was the strangest day of my life,' he says. 'I looked around to my left and right, trying to absorb the noises and work out where I was. *Where am I?* Just total confusion. I had a head full of fluff'.

But the main thing was that Muamba was still alive!

But, could he go on to make a full, miraculous recovery? The football world was supporting him all the way. His former Arsenal teammate Thierry Henry came to visit him in hospital, while in Spain, Lionel Messi warmed up for Barcelona's match against Granada wearing a T-shirt with the words: 'FABRICE!!!! WE ARE BEHIND YOU.'

Inspired by all the kind messages from players and fans, Muamba bounced back brilliantly. One week later, his heart was beating properly again, and he could move his arms and legs, and two weeks later, he was sitting up in his hospital bed, with a big smile on his face. And why not? Because although he would never be able to play professional football again, Muamba simply felt lucky to still be alive.

Soon, he was up and walking, and after a month in hospital, he was able to go home. By 5 May 2012, he was even well enough to go to the Reebok Stadium to watch a very special football match: Bolton Wanderers versus Tottenham Hotspur, but this time, in the Premier League.

Of course, Muamba wished he could be playing. But just being out there on the pitch again and hearing so many fans clapping and chanting his name was an incredible feeling.

'Thank you from the bottom of my heart,' he said on that very emotional night. 'Thank you – not just the Bolton fans but the whole country. The support has been overwhelming and I'm just grateful I can walk again and do things normally again.'

Muamba's biggest thanks, however, went to the medical heroes who saved his life – Tobin, the team at the London Chest Hospital, and Deaner, the doctor in the stands who had played such a massive part on the pitch.

**'The NHS is unbelievable – so good, it takes my breath away. Paramedics, doctors, the guys who drive the ambulances, the nurses and everyone else deserve more credit and more thanks than I can ever express. They are the real heroes in society. They are the real heroes in my story too.'**

Do you want to know one final weird and wonderful fact about this unbelievable football story? Deaner wasn't even supposed to be there at the game. He was only there because his nephew couldn't go, and so there was a spare ticket!

'There is always that thought of, *What if he wasn't there that day?*' Muamba said in 2022, on the tenth anniversary of that match. 'Andrew did a great job of being in the right place at the right time. He took over when I was in the ambulance. He made sure I was taken care of.'

These days, Muamba is back at Bolton, working as the coach of the club's Under-15 team. And Deaner? Well, he's still watching from the stands at Tottenham, always ready to help and become a football hero again.

## The Filipinas Who Wowed the Women's Football World

After two tales of non-sporting drama, it's time for some proper football action. I'm talking last-minute match-winners, stunning penalty shoot-out saves, shock World Cup wins, and not one but twenty-three unlikely football heroes. Sound exciting? Good, welcome to the wonderful world of the Philippines women's national football team.

The Philippines is a country in Southeast Asia, best known for its beautiful beaches, amazing volcanoes, and delicious street food. Fun fact: their national bird is the monkey-eating eagle, or Philippine eagle. (Yes, that is a real bird. No, they don't actually eat monkeys – but they do eat snakes and pigs . . . Eesh!)

It's made up of lots of little islands – 7,641 of them to be exact. Put together, they form a country with a population of more than 115 million people (double the population of England). But football is probably only the fourth most popular sport there, behind basketball, boxing and volleyball.

Despite that, the Philippines women's football team played their first international match way back in 1981. That day, they lost 2–0 against Hong Kong, and since then, they've experienced a lot more lows than highs. In 1995, they lost 21–0 against China, and in 2007, FIFA ranked them as the 92nd best national team in the world . . . out of only 144. Ouch!

But, ten years later, the Philippines had grand ambitions for the future: they wanted to qualify for the FIFA Women's World Cup for the first time.

The next tournament was coming up in 2019 – could the Philippines achieve their goal and become one of the twenty-four teams competing in France? To do so, they would have to finish in the top five at the 2018 AFC (Asian Football Confederation) Women's Asian Cup in Jordan. That might not sound too bad at first, but here are some facts you need to know:

1. Australia, China, Japan and South Korea all competed in the AFC Women's Asian Cup, so that was four places pretty much filled already

2. This was the first time the Philippines had qualified for the AFC Women's Asian Cup since 2006

Hmmm, doesn't sound so easy now, eh? The Philippines Football Federation (PFF) decided that it was time to get serious, and so they set up 'Project Jordan'.

The plan was simple: **better organisation, better training and better players.**

That last part was definitely the most difficult. They had already found the most talented footballers in the Philippines and were working hard to improve them, so the next step was to start scouting in other countries. Since the 1970s, millions of people had been leaving the Philippines to go to the USA, Australia and Europe – and now their children were growing up in those places, playing high-quality football. It was just a case of finding them and persuading them to join the national team!

The Philippines hired a new coach called Richard

Boon, who had experience of working in US women's soccer. Then, once the new squad had been selected, the team got together for an intense, three-month training camp ahead of the 2018 AFC Women's Asian Cup.

So, did 'Project Jordan' get the job done? No, not straight away. Unfortunately, the Philippines finished third in their group behind China and their big rivals, Thailand. That was enough to earn them a World Cup playoff spot, but in that crucial game, they were thrashed 5–0 by South Korea. Their 2019 Women's World Cup dream was officially over. Oh well, on to the next one . . .

The good news for the Philippines was that an extra eight teams would qualify for the 2023 tournament, including one more country from the Asian Football Confederation.

The bad news was that the Philippines team was far from a well-oiled winning-machine. After finishing a disappointing fourth at the 2019 Southeast Asian

Games, they didn't play a single match until September 2021 due to COVID-19. Nearly two years without any international football – it's not exactly a recipe for success, is it?

But what the players lacked in form and fitness, they certainly made up for in skill and spirit. In the Asian Cup qualifiers, the Philippines scored two late goals to beat Nepal, and then another to defeat Hong Kong. Yesssss, they were on their way to the Asian Cup!

There, in their very first group game, they faced their biggest local rivals. The Philippines had lost their last thirteen matches against Thailand, but now, under new Australian manager Alen Stajcic, they were a different team. The young players brought together by 'Project Jordan' were getting better and better: captain Tahnai Annis, speedy attackers Quinley Quezada and Sarina Bolden, and the McDaniel sisters, Olivia (goalkeeper) and Chandler (striker). Although they were all born in the USA, their mums were proud Filipinas, and therefore, so were they.

After 80 minutes of hard-fought action, it was Chandler McDaniel who scored the winner, firing a long-range strike past the Thailand keeper. *GOAL!*

They had done it! With huge smiles on their faces, the Philippines players celebrated a famous victory together. Then, six days later, they won again, thrashing Indonesia 6–0 to make it through to the quarter-finals. Wow, they were now just one step away from securing a spot at the 2023 Women's World Cup!

Against Chinese Taipei, the Philippines got off to a great start and they took the lead early in the second half. Hurray, they were almost there now!

But with less than ten minutes to go, Zhuo Li-ping curled an unstoppable shot over Olivia McDaniel and into the top corner. Nooooooo – 1–1! After 30 nervy minutes of extra-time, the match went all the way to penalties.

Oooooh, what drama!

When Chinese Taipei scored their first three spot-kicks, it really didn't look good for the Philippines, but don't worry, there was still time for their keeper to save the day. Olivia McDaniel dived down to save one penalty, then another, and she even stepped up and scored one herself! It was all up to Bolden now. She ran up and . . . slammed the ball into the bottom corner.

The Filipinas had won the shoot-out! From 92nd in the world, they were now into the Asian Cup semi-finals. AND they were about to become the first Philippines team to appear at a major international football tournament – the World Cup! There were absolute SCENES after that, as the players hugged, sang, danced, and cried happy tears together.

The Philippines lost 2–0 to South Korea in the Asia Cup semi-finals, but as one exciting adventure ended, another one began. '2023 Women's World Cup, here we come!' the Filipinas cried.

They went into the tournament with confidence, but winning at the World Cup was going to be a much greater challenge. In their opening game, they lost 2–0 against a strong Switzerland team, and next up they faced one of the tournament hosts, New Zealand, who had already beaten Norway.

As the underdogs, the Filipinas still went into the next match with nothing to lose. In the team huddle before kick-off, the players cheered with passion and pride, and after 24 minutes, they were jumping for joy. From wide on the right, midfielder Sara Eggesvik curled a brilliant cross into the box, and there was Bolden, jumping up high above two defenders to head the ball into the net. *1–0!*

Wow! As the home crowd went silent, the much smaller group of Filipina fans went wild and so did the millions of supporters back home, all singing a special song for their scorer. She was already a national hero, but now she was a national SUPER-hero:

*Sar-in-a Bolden, na na na na na na!*

*Sar-in-a Bolden, na na na na na na!*

What a moment – now, could they hold on for a famous first World Cup victory?

In the second half, New Zealand attacked again and again, but the Filipinas stuck to their task and defended fiercely, with sliding tackles, powerful headers, brave blocks and super saves. In the 92nd minute, a New Zealand forward volleyed the ball towards the bottom corner, but out flew Olivia McDaniel's left glove to tip it past the post. Phew!

Seconds later, McDaniel kicked the ball high into the air, and the final whistle blew – New Zealand 0, Philippines 1. What a performance and what a story. They had battled through disappointments, lockdowns and penalty drama to make it all the way to their first Women's World Cup and then to their first World Cup **WIN!**

Unfortunately, the Philippines lost their next match against Norway and were knocked out of the World Cup. But it didn't matter – their players returned home as heroes. The Filipinas were now history-makers, every single one of them.

'WE'RE JUST DOING SOMETHING WE LOVE, BUT TO BE ABLE TO HAVE THIS BIG OF AN IMPACT FOR THE COUNTRY AND TO HELP THOSE LITTLE GIRLS WHO ARE LIKE, *I WANT TO DO THAT*, AND BRING PEOPLE INTO SPORTS AND TO HELP SOCCER GROW, IT'S AN HONOUR TO BE ABLE TO DO THAT FOR THE COUNTRY.'

– Chandler McDaniel

# The Two Watches of Diego Maradona

One minute on the stopwatch . . . go!

Maradona, an attacking midfielder from Argentina and an absolute football genius, was one of the greatest players of all time. Diego sadly died in 2020 at the age of only 60, but his legend lives on. He's best remembered for his magical performances at the 1986 World Cup, where he led his national team all the way to the trophy with his super-skilful left foot (and super-sneaky left hand!).

But as well as being a football icon, Diego has always been a style icon too. On the pitch, the Argentinian was known for his short shorts, his Puma King boots, and his very healthy head of bushy, black hair. And off the pitch, he was known for wearing lots of flashy jewellery: diamond earrings, silver bracelets, chunky gold chains . . . and two matching watches at the same time!

Yes, really! Find a photo of Diego not dressed in football kit and I'll bet you'll find a watch on each wrist.

But why? Was it to:

A) Balance himself out (those pricey watches can be pretty heavy, you know!)?

B) Always know the time in Italy, as well as in Argentina?

C) Remind Napoli fans of the number of Serie A titles that he helped the club win in the 1980s?

D) Remind England fans of the number of goals he scored against them for Argentina in the 1986 World Cup quarter-finals (and one of them with his hand, as well!)?

And the answer is . . . no one really knows for sure, and sadly, Diego is no longer alive to tell us. Sorry!

But I believe a story told by one of the world's most famous watchmakers. The boss of Hublot, Ricardo Guadalupe, said, 'He told me he wore two watches because he has two daughters . . . And we always had to engrave the watches – one with one daughter's name and one with the other's.'

Awww. The names of Diego's daughters are Dalma and Gianinna. Dalma is a famous actor in Argentina, while Gianinna is a fashion designer who married another famous footballer, former Manchester City striker Sergio Agüero. Gianinna and Sergio's son, Benjamin, is now fifteen years old, and he has a lot to live up to. His granddad is Maradona, his dad is Agüero, and oh, his godfather is Lionel Messi! Will Benjamin become the next football superstar in the family? Only time will tell, but he has a couple of his grandfather's watches to help with that.

# CHAPTER TWO

# INCREDIBLE COMEBACKS

Agonising accidents, frustrating form, disappointing defeats, disastrous debuts – the list of sporting setbacks is never-ending, but that's enough about the bad stuff. Instead, we're going to **focus on the positives**, not the negatives – the comebacks, not the comedowns. Because as 'the King of Football', Pelé, himself once said, **'The more difficult the victory, the greater the happiness in winning.'**

In this next section, we're celebrating the **inspiring stories** of football players and teams who have been knocked down, but got back up again to achieve even more amazing things. So, get ready to have your heart warmed and your love of the game taken to a whole new level . . .

## The 'One-Handed God' Who Won the World Cup

*30 July 1930, Estadio Centenario, Montevideo, Uruguay*

With two minutes to go in the first-ever World Cup final, the hosts Uruguay are winning 3–2 against their South American rivals Argentina. Is there still time for one final goal? Yes, but it's not the Argentina equaliser that most of the 93,000 supporters in the stadium are fearing. Instead, Uruguay move the ball up the pitch on the counter-attack and one of their forwards smashes it into the roof of the net. *GOAL!*

Game over. Uruguay are the winners – the first Football Champions of the World! There were joyful celebrations all over the country that night, and all the next day too; it was even declared a national holiday. But this story isn't really about that exciting match. It's about the scorer of that final World Cup-winning goal –

Héctor Castro, the Uruguayan footballer nicknamed *'El Divino Manco'* or 'The One-Handed God' in English.

Why? Because he only had one hand! Yes, as you're about to find out, Castro's life was full of painful setbacks and incredible comebacks.

OK, let's get the gory bit out the way first. Castro was born in 1904 in Montevideo, Uruguay's capital city. One day, aged thirteen, as he was cutting wood with an electric saw, Castro was involved in a horrible accident where he lost the lower part of his right arm, up past the elbow. Owwwwwwww!

It was an awful tragedy. One where most people might have given up all hope of playing high-level sport, but not Castro. He wasn't going to let anything stop him from chasing his dream. In those days, there was no such thing as Paralympic or disability sport. But he still had his other arm and he figured football was a game played with the feet, anyway!

He still had everything he needed to succeed – strength, a powerful shot and a clever football brain

– and so, as soon as he could, Castro began his first football comeback. At the age of seventeen, he signed for local team Club Atlético Lito. Then two impressive years later in 1923, he joined Nacional, one of Uruguay's two most successful clubs, along with Peñarol.

It was a big step-up for such a young player, but Castro made it look simple. What he lacked in dribbling skills and style, he made up for in effort and goal-scoring instinct. He went straight into the Nacional starting line-up and played so well that he stayed there, helping them win the Uruguayan league title in his first season. Hurray, he was a trophy-winning football hero already!

But what about his missing right forearm – didn't Castro's limb difference make it harder for him to become a football star? Sometimes it did, but he was determined to succeed, even if that sometimes meant sneakily using his half-arm to his advantage. When he jumped up in the air to try to win headers, he would often whack opponents out of the way with it! According to football writer Alfie Potts Harmer, *El Divino Manco* was devilishly clever in and around the box, but considered by many to even be quite a dirty player.'

The Nacional fans didn't care about that, though. In fact, they loved Castro's strength and fighting spirit, and soon so did the supporters of the Uruguay national team. Castro made his debut for La Celeste ('The Sky Blue' because of the colour of their kit) in 1923, and three years later, he scored six goals as they won the 1926 South American Football Championship (these days called the 'Copa América').

By then, Uruguay was seen as the best national team in not just South America, but the whole wide world! They had already won Olympic Gold in 1924, though Castro hadn't been selected in the squad that time. But could he help them win a second in 1928? That was the aim as La Celeste set off on a trip to the Netherlands.

Castro was selected and he scored one of the goals as Uruguay thrashed Germany 4–1 in the Olympic quarter-finals. Surely that would be enough to secure his place as one of their starting forwards for the rest of the tournament? No, sadly the Uruguay squad was so strong that he didn't even get to play in the final, where they beat Argentina!

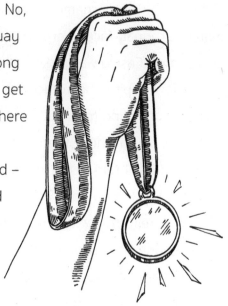

Oh well, never mind – Castro still got a gold medal, and he was a strong character who never got too down about disappointments. He had bounced back after his awful arm accident, and he would do it again . . .

Just as Uruguay's Olympic adventure came to a successful end, an exciting new adventure began. After years of discussion, FIFA decided it was finally time to hold a separate world competition, just for football – and as the two-time gold medallists, Uruguay were selected to host the first World Cup!

In 1930, the tournament began. In their first group match, Uruguay faced Peru, and after a strong season at Nacional, Castro was picked as one of the team's five forwards. Despite the attacking 2-3-5 formation, the game was heading for a 0–0 draw until *El Divino Manco* saved the day. In the 65th minute, he used his devilishly clever football-brain to fire in the winner and Uruguay's first-ever World Cup goal. What a hero!

Now, surely that would be enough to secure Castro's place as one of their starting forwards for the rest of the tournament? No, again sadly the Uruguay squad was just too strong. Back came star striker Peregrino Anselmo, who scored one against Romania and then two in their semi-final win over Yugoslavia.

Oh dear, it looked like *El Divino Manco* was going to miss out on another major tournament final . . . or was he? Some reports say Anselmo was ill, others say injured, but whatever the reason, he wasn't fit to play in the final against their fierce rivals Argentina. And so, it was time for Castro's most incredible comeback of all!

As the big match approached, however, he still had a few more obstacles to overcome. There were rumours that Castro and some of his teammates were offered huge amounts of money to help Argentina win. Then, the night before the final, he received a mysterious phone call, saying he would 'never enjoy another sunset' if Uruguay won.

Eesh! Now, Castro might have been a slightly dirty player sometimes, but he wasn't a cheat and he wasn't afraid of anyone or anything. An electric saw cutting off half his right arm hadn't stopped him from chasing his football dream, so money and death threats weren't going to make any difference at all. He was determined to come back and lead Uruguay to World Cup glory, and as you know from the beginning of this story, he did exactly that. In fact, he put on a classic Castro performance, fouling the Argentina keeper in the first half, and then scoring the game-winning goal late in the second. When the final whistle blew, Castro was lifted up and carried around the stadium by supporters. *El Divino*

*Manco* had done it. 'The One-Handed God' had won the World Cup.

**FUN FACT:** In 1930, the rivalry between Uruguay and Argentina was so fierce that both teams refused to play the World Cup final with a ball chosen by the other. In the end, FIFA had to come up with a clever compromise: for the first half, they would use Argentina's ball, and then for the second, Uruguay's!

The Red Dragons Who Came Roaring Back [With a Little Help from Hollywood!]

Next up, we have the unbelievable bounceback story of the third-oldest professional football club in the world:

1. Notts County, founded 1862
2. Stoke City, founded 1863
3. **Wrexham Association Football Club, founded 1864!**

Wrexham is a small city in North East Wales, close to the English border and 40 miles from Liverpool. And Wrexham's football team? Well, the history of 'the Red Dragons' may be long, but it isn't exactly overflowing with success . . .

**Trophies (not including Welsh cups and league titles):**

> **Only four in 156 years** including the Football League North Cup 1943–44, Third Division Champions 1977–78, Football League Trophy

2004–05 and FA Trophy 2012–13

For those who like maths, that's 39 years per trophy!

**Highest-ever league position:**

> **Fifteenth in the Second Division** (now called the 'EFL Championship'), **1978–79**
>
> **Promotions:** five
>
> **Relegations:** seven

It was a sad story and it seemed to be getting sadder with every season. When Wrexham suffered their last relegation in 2008, they dropped out of the EFL for the first time, and had been stuck playing non-league football ever since.

In 2019–20, the club slipped to nineteenth in the National League, their lowest-ever finish, and it could have been even worse. If the season hadn't been suspended because of COVID-19, they might have got relegated . . . again! Oof, Wrexham were going through a tough time, both on and off the pitch. Since 2011, the club had been owned by a group of fans called the Wrexham Supporters Trust, but money was tight and spirits were low.

Across the Atlantic Ocean in Philadelphia, USA, actor and sports fan Rob McElhenney was stuck at home and looking for a new TV series to watch. A friend from England, Humphrey Ker, had a recommendation for him: *Sunderland 'Til I Die*. Hmm, a documentary about a struggling football club that he had never even heard of? McElhenney wasn't sure at first, but after a few episodes, he was hooked. What a programme, what a place, and what passion the people had for their local football team! McElhenney sent a message to Ker:

**'I love this. We should do something like this. We should buy a club. We should make a documentary. Can we buy a football club? Which could we buy?'**

The answers to McElhenney's questions were:

1.  Yes, if you really want to!
2.  A club that isn't doing very well

As a millionaire, rather than a billionaire, McElhenney couldn't afford to buy one of the big Premier League clubs. Instead, he was in the market for an old club with a long history and a loyal fanbase, which found itself struggling in the lower leagues . . .

Notts County? No, they had just been bought by Danish brothers Alexander and Christoffer Reedtz.

Stoke City? No, they were flying high in the Championship.

OK, so what about . . . Wrexham? Long history? *Tick!* Their stadium, the Racecourse Ground ('*Y Cae Ras*' in Welsh), built in 1801 was the world's oldest international football stadium that still hosted matches. Loyal fanbase? *Tick!* Even in the National League, Wrexham still got crowds of more than four thousand fans for every home game.

McElhenney was keen to know more. He then got in touch with a very famous (and very rich) friend, the actor Ryan Reynolds (the *Deadpool* guy, if that helps). Would he be interested in teaming up to bring the good times back to Wrexham AFC? Yes, he would!

When the Wrexham fans heard the news that some

Americans wanted to buy their club, the reaction was a mix of, *Amazing, that's just what we need!* and *Noooo, not this again!* Two businessmen had bought the club before, back in 2002, but despite promising to make Wrexham stronger, they had nearly destroyed it. The fans couldn't afford to let that happen again.

These mystery Americans weren't messing around, though. They were serious about helping the Red Dragons climb back up into the English Football League. But it wasn't all about success on the pitch; it was about helping the local community bounce back too.

In November 2020, their identities were revealed: Hollywood stars McElhenney and Reynolds were making an offer to buy Wrexham for about £2 million, despite never even visiting the club. Really? Yes! By February 2021, the deal was done.

Could this dream-team get the Red Dragons roaring back up the football leagues? Not straight away, no. When McElhenney and Reynolds took over mid-season, Wrexham were twelfth, and when the season ended four months later, they had only moved up four places to eighth, still one place below the play-off spots. Oh well, they were staying in the National League, at least for one more year . . .

With the season over, McElhenney and Reynolds could now really get to work, turning Wrexham's fortunes around. They brought in:

- A new manager – Phil Parkinson, the former boss of Bradford City, Bolton Wanderers and Sunderland
- A new kit sponsor – the massive social media company TikTok
- A load of new players – including defenders Ben Tozer and Aaron Hayden, midfielder James Jones, giant forward Ollie Palmer, and most famously, sharp-shooting striker Paul Mullin

'Promotion, promotion, promotion is Wrexham's aim,' Reynolds declared as the 2021–22 campaign kicked off.

With so many new faces at the club, the Red Dragons took a while to hit top form, but once they did, they flew up the table – tenth to seventh to fifth to second!

Unfortunately, they couldn't quite catch the National League leaders Stockport County. Only the top team got automatic promotion to League Two, and so Wrexham had to enter the play-offs instead, where they lost 5–4 in extra-time against Grimsby Town. Nooooooo.

It was a crushing blow, but what brilliant drama for the TV documentary! When the first series of *Welcome to Wrexham* came out in 2022, it was a huge hit and suddenly, the club had thousands of new fans and the city had thousands of new visitors who had fallen in love with the place and the local people.

But back to the football . . .

New season, same goal: promotion, promotion, promotion! To help with that, Wrexham made more new signings, including speedy wing-back Jacob Mendy and skilful midfield playmaker Elliot Lee. The Red Dragons were determined to finish top of the league this time!

It wasn't going to be easy, though, because Wrexham weren't the only team winning game after game after game:

12 November 2022

*1. Notts County – 44 points*

*2. Wrexham – 43 points . . .*

11 February 2023

*1. Wrexham – 78 points*

*2. Notts County – 77 points . . .*

7 April 2023

*1. Notts County – 100 points*

*2. Wrexham – 100 points . . .*

On and on went the battle at the top until finally the two old clubs met at the Racecourse Ground on 10 April 2023 for a tense title decider.

In their biggest game in years, Wrexham went 1–0 down just before half-time, but they fought back through goals from Mullin, Mendy and Lee to lead 3–2 with seconds to go. The entertainment wasn't over yet, though. No, like the best Hollywood movies, there was still more late drama to come. In the 95th minute, a cross came into the box and struck defender Eoghan O'Connell on the arm. *Handball – penalty to Notts County!*

Wow, what a nerve-wracking moment for Wrexham and their 39-year-old keeper Ben Foster. The former England international had only recently joined the club but now he had an early chance to become a Wrexham hero! Could he take it?

Up stepped Cedwyn Scott, who fired a fierce low shot towards the bottom corner . . .

Foster dived down . . . And saved it!

A mighty roar went up, from the fans, the players and the owners. For McElhenney and Reynolds, buying a British football club might have started out as a business move, but now they were both totally hooked on the beautiful game.

'THAT WAS UNLIKE ANYTHING I'VE EVER SEEN BEFORE. WHEN I GET MY HANDS ON BEN FOSTER, HE'S GOING TO BE ON THE INJURED LIST BECAUSE I'M GOING TO BREAK RIBS, I'M GOING TO HUG HIM SO HARD!'

– Ryan Reynolds

With that incredible win, Wrexham moved clear of Notts County at the top, and after two more victories, the National League title was theirs. Finally, a fifth trophy! And after fifteen long years of disappointment, the Red Dragons were roaring back to the EFL at last!

First stop: League Two, but Wrexham refused to stay there long. In their very first season, they fired their way straight up to League One, and the club is aiming a lot higher for the future: 'I see this as a march towards the Premier League,' McElhenney said back in 2023. 'None of us thinks that's going to be easy. But whether it takes five years, or whether it takes twenty years, that's the goal.'

And with a little help from Hollywood, why not? One thing's for sure, though: there'll be plenty more drama in Wrexham along the way.

# The Remarkable Return of Mary Queen of Stops

They say everyone deserves a second chance, and in football, that feels especially true for goalkeepers. As the last line of a team's defence, any mistakes they make can look MASSIVE, like they're being studied under a ginormous microscope. The hero of this story hadn't made mistakes – certainly nothing huge or obvious, anyway – and yet at one international match in November 2019, Mary Earps was England's first-choice keeper, and three days later, she was not.

Why? What had she done wrong?

The answer wasn't clear, but when it came to the SheBelieves Cup in March 2020, the Lionesses manager Phil Neville selected three keepers in his squad: the experienced Carly Telford and young future stars Ellie Roebuck and Sandy MacIver.

'What about me?' Mary wondered. After years of watching and waiting from the bench, it seemed like Earps' big moment as number 1 had come and gone already.

The next few years were a real struggle. First, club football was suspended due to COVID-19, and then, when it returned and Earps performed well, England didn't come calling again. She was keeping Manchester United up near the top of the WSL table – what more could she do? To make matters even worse, in 2021, when United offered her a new contract, the money was so low that she wasn't sure it would be enough to even pay her bills.

'I got to a point where I felt I had sort of reached my limits,' Earps admitted later.

As she described it in another interview, her career felt 'dead and gone. Run over

three thousand times and trampled by elephants.'

So, was it time for Mary to give up on the beautiful game, the sport she had loved since she was an eight-year-old girl kicking a ball around with her dad and brother in the garden? She had studied hard at university to get a business degree – was that what she should do instead?

Earps thought long and hard about it, but in the end, after advice from her family and the Manchester United men's keeper David de Gea, she decided to give her football career a couple more years.

Phew! Thank goodness for that, because there were really good times ahead for Earps. As the England song 'Sweet Caroline' says:

### *SO GOOD, SO GOOD, SO GOOD!*

In September 2021, Dutch coach Sarina Wiegman became the new England women's manager, and according to Earps, 'Life changed just like that. I felt that she really understood where I came from and had real empathy for me as a human being.'

Yes, when Sarina announced her squad for the first match against North Macedonia, there was a surprise name amongst the shot-stoppers:

Telford, MacIver . . . and Earps. Mary was BACK! Not only that but after nearly two years of missed matches, she was also back in the starting line-up.

Now that she had the England number 1 shirt back, Earps was determined to keep it. After a clean sheet against North Macedonia (8–0), she kept more against:

- Luxembourg (10–0)
- Northern Ireland (4–0)
- Latvia (10–0)
- Austria (1–0)
- Latvia, again (20–0)

Wow, what a remarkable return! In February 2022, England did finally concede their first goal under Sarina, but only one and it was a stunning strike from Canada's Janine Beckie that flew into the top corner. Unstoppable! Earps wasn't going to lose her place over that one. She was officially England's number 1 now.

And the even more exciting news? The next Euros were coming up soon! Mary had been to two major international tournaments before, but only as the third-choice keeper, watching from the bench. This time, she would be out there in goal, wearing the gloves for her country.

When the tournament kicked off, Earps' remarkable return continued. Now that she had a boss who believed in her, she felt like a superhero, flying to the rescue again and again. In their opening game against Austria, she dived down brilliantly to save Barbara Dunst's shot and help England hold on for a 1–0 win. But after that, in the group stage, it was over to the attackers:

*England 8 Norway 0*

*England 5 Northern Ireland 0*

Three games, three clean sheets – all hail 'Mary Queen of Stops'! And she was only just getting started . . .

In the quarter-final against Spain, there was nothing Earps could do about Esther González's opening goal,

but later on, she made a fantastic fingertip-save to keep England in the game, which they eventually won in extra-time.

In the semi-final against Sweden, she made three crucial early stops before England ran away to a 4–0 win, and Earps kept her best for the final at Wembley against Germany.

In the first half, when the ball bounced loose in the England box, she threw her body down and grabbed it. *SAVE!*

Then in the second, when Lina Magull blasted a rocket of a shot towards the top corner, she jumped up high and somehow managed to tip it on to the bar. *SAVE!*

The ball bounced out to Lea Schüller, who went for the volley . . . but Earps got back up to stop that too. *DOUBLE SAVE!*

The girl from Nottingham was having the time of her life in goal for her country, and when Chloe Kelly scored the winner in extra-time, her bounceback year got even better. From an England nobody, Earps was now a European Champion! Surely, her life and football career couldn't get much better than that?

No, it could! Earps continued her fantastic form for Manchester United, leading them to the UEFA Women's Champions League and becoming the first keeper in the WSL to reach 150 starts and 50 clean sheets. She even broke the record by keeping fourteen of them in a row!

And for England? Well, Earps took her game to an even higher level in 2023.

In April, the Lionesses faced Brazil in the Women's 'Finalissima', a new match between the champions of Europe and South America. England scored first but Brazil scored a late equaliser, and so the trophy was decided by . . . duh-duh-duh – PENALTIES!

There was no need to worry though, because the Lionesses had an ice-cold keeper who was determined to save the day. Earps couldn't quite stop Adriana's first spot-kick, but she flung herself across her goal to tip the next strike from Tamires around the post. *Saved!*

'Come onnnnnnnn!' roared Mary Queen of Stops.

Five spot-kicks later, Chloe Kelly stepped up and scored the winner, and as they celebrated, all the Lionesses rushed over to thank their incredible keeper. Captain Leah Williamson even asked Earps to lift the trophy with her, holding one arm each!

The Euros? *Tick!* The Finalissima? *Tick!* Could England now complete the hat-trick by winning the World Cup held in

Australia and New Zealand too?

They won their first two matches:

*England 1 Haiti 0*

*England 1 Denmark 0*

Next up, China and England. It took a penalty from China's Wang Shuang to finally get past Mary Queen of Stops, but it didn't matter, England won 6–1! And after that, Earps went straight back to being unbeatable:

*England 0 Nigeria 0*

In the quarter-finals, Colombia took the lead after a brilliant chip from Leicy Santos, but England bounced back to win 2–1, with Mary making a super-save to stop a long-range shot from Lorena Bedoya.

Yessss, Lionesses! England were through to the World Cup semi-finals, and this time, they had made it through to the final at last, with a 3–1 win over Australia.

Now, could England go all the way and lift the World Cup trophy?

Just like at Wembley against Germany a year earlier, Earps saved her best for the final.

She bravely blocked shots from Alba Redondo and Salma Paralluelo . . .

. . . she tipped another from Mariona Caldentey around the post . . .

. . . she used her legs to stop a strike from Ona Batlle.

And best of all, she dived down to save a penalty from Jenni Hermoso.

What a stunning performance! And yet it still wasn't enough to stop Spain from winning the final 1–0.

It was a heartbreaking end to a terrific tournament, for England and especially for Earps, their heroic number 1. But after so long working away in the shadows of women's football, she was now in the spotlight at last, and the awards were flooding in:

- FIFA Women's World Cup Golden Glove
- FIFA Women's Goalkeeper of the Year
- England Women's Player of the Year
- BBC Women's Footballer of the Year
- *Sunday Times* Sportswoman of the Year

Well done and well-deserved, Mary – bet you're glad you didn't give up on football back in 2021, eh? We fans certainly are!

# The (LEGO) Houses that Arminia Bielefeld Built

So far in this section, we've focused on the most famous meaning of the word 'comeback' – *'recovering from a setback like a total (football) superstar'*. For this last story, however, we're going to look at another meaning of that word – *'a sharp or witty reply'*.

The year is 1996, and Giuseppe Reina is a young German striker on the rise. After scoring ten goals for SG Wattenscheid 09 in his country's second division, he now has teams in the top division wanting to sign him. Arminia Bielefeld have just been promoted and they need a new striker – perfect!

The two clubs quickly agree a transfer fee of €375,000, but when it comes to his contract, Reina decides to try his luck and include a very unusual request: 'I want you to build me a new house for every year that I stay at the club.'

What?! Talk about making yourself at home, eh? But weirdly, instead of laughing in Reina's face and telling him to get lost, Arminia Bielefeld accept his request.

Again, what?! But Reina doesn't ask any more questions. He joins the club, thinking he's just signed the best contract EVER, and happily scores eight goals in his first season. Right, where's that new house then?

Are you ready for Arminia Bielefeld's comeback? Reina certainly wasn't. Although the contract said the club owed him a house, it didn't say how big it had to be, or what it had to be made of. So, instead of a real house, they present Reina with a lovely little house . . . made of LEGO bricks!

Ta-da! As you can probably imagine, the striker didn't see the funny side of that. In fact, he threw his toys out of the pram (geddit?!) and took Arminia Bielefeld to court over the three ACTUAL, FULL-SIZED houses he claimed they owed him. In the end, the club agreed to give Reina some money instead, and after three years, he moved home to join Borussia Dortmund, where he won the league title in 2002. I wonder if he asked for any weird bonuses in that contract too . . .

The moral of this story is: always read something carefully before you sign it. Or, if you can't be bothered, don't make ridiculous requests in the first place!

# CHAPTER THREE

# HELP! NEW PLAYERS NEEDED

Here's a pretty obvious football fact for you: in order to win a match, it really helps to have your best players on the pitch.

In an ideal world, you'd have all eleven of them out there together, but as you're about to read, the world of football isn't always perfect. Sometimes, things go wrong or get in the way – **injuries, red cards, military service, war, COVID-19** – but whatever happens, everyone's favourite game **MUST GO ON!** Even if you have to find new football heroes from unlikely places . . .

# A Christmas Day to Forget for the Seagulls

Finding eleven fit and available footballers is never an easy job, but on Christmas Day during the Second World War? That would be a seriously tricky task, wouldn't it?

The war began in September 1939, when Adolf Hitler's invasion of Poland led British Prime Minister Neville Chamberlain to declare war on Nazi Germany. On the same day, the government also passed a conscription bill, which meant all males aged eighteen to forty-one had to sign up for military service.

All males aged eighteen to forty-one? Well, that took away almost every single player in the entire English Football League, and they had no choice but to abandon the 1939–40 season. After that, official club football stayed suspended until the war was over in 1946. But completely stopping people from playing the world's most popular sport? You can't – it's impossible! And so, despite everything else that was happening, games did still go on during those difficult years in between.

Soon, a special new league called the 'Wartime League' was set up, and the seventy teams who joined were split into two massive divisions: the North Regional Championship (any club based above the Midlands) and the South Regional Championship, where this particular unbelievable story takes place on 25 December 1940.

That year, the government asked people to only travel if absolutely necessary, and most of Britain was preparing for a very quiet Christmas Day at home. But not the footballers. An exception was made for them – after all, what better way to keep the morale of the people up, other than a good game of footie!

Leicester City and Northampton Town played each other TWICE that day – one match at each club's stadium. Meanwhile, the players and coaches of Brighton and Hove Albion Football Club had a much longer journey to make. For some weird and wonderful reason, the

Wartime League had arranged for 'the Seagulls', a team from England's south coast, to make a 350-mile round trip to play against Norwich City, a team based midway up the east coast. Why on Christmas Day? Don't ask me! Fun festive entertainment, I guess . . .

The Brighton manager Charlie Webb hopped on the train on Christmas Eve, along with four of his players: one from the first team (Joe Wilson) and three from the youth team (Roy Watts, Charlie Chase and Charlie Harman).

*OK, but what about the other seven players?* you might be wondering. Well, they were supposed to meet them in Norwich, but can you guess what happened? Yep, they didn't turn up in time (there was a war going on, remember!).

With kick-off fast approaching, Brighton still only had four players. Oh well, should they just call off the game and go home for some Christmas dinner? Wartime

matches were being cancelled all the time, mainly because of missing players doing military service, but also because of dangerous conditions. And no, I don't mean bad weather – a few months earlier, Brighton's match at Southampton had been abandoned three minutes into the game when air-raid sirens signalled that the German air force, the *Luftwaffe*, were about to attack.

So back to Christmas Day 1940 – Norwich were quite happy to stay in the warm and give the match a miss, but Brighton? No, there was no way their manager Webb was giving up that easily. They couldn't just disappoint the fans who were looking forward to watching a football match, and besides, Brighton held the proud record of never cancelling a wartime game. They weren't going to change that now.

But where were they going to find seven players in a hurry? There was only one answer: Carrow Road, the stadium where the match was taking place! According to Harman, one of 'the Brighton Four', 'Before the game, stewards went round the ground appealing for players and listing the various vacant positions: goalkeeper, and so on.'

**'HELP, new players needed!'**

Wow, what an incredible Christmas gift for any aspiring footballers in the crowd – the chance to get involved in the game! Surprise, surprise, there were plenty of volunteers, and so this is the Brighton team that eventually took to the field:

1. ***A. Bartram*** *– a random man picked from the crowd*
2. ***Roy Watts***
3. ***F. Pinchbeck*** *– random man number two*
4. ***Charlie Chase***
5. ***Jimmy Ithell*** *– a player on loan from Bolton Wanderers for the day*
6. ***Derek Dye*** *– a Norwich youth player that Brighton were allowed to borrow*
7. ***Charlie Harman***
8. ***S. Bird*** *– random man number three*
9. ***W.A. Stacey*** *– random man number four*

**10.** *Joe Wilson*

**11.** *A. Smith* – *random man number five*

There you have it – Brighton's all-star team of wise men for Christmas Day! And how did they do? Not very well, I'm afraid. Not very well at all. But before we talk about the actual scoreline, let's get a couple more excuses out of the way first:

1. Norwich were a really good team! In the two South Regional League matches before this one, they had scored thirteen goals and only conceded one. Up front, they had Fred Chadwick, who was one of the best available strikers in Britain at the time.

2. 'I don't know who he was but the goalkeeper who played for us was hopeless' – Charlie Harman (Poor Mr A. Bartram – your team did ask for extra players from the crowd, Charlie!)

OK, enough excuses – let's get on to the action. Cheered on by nearly 1,500 fans, Brighton started the game like a team of strangers with varying levels of football talent and fitness. Oh wait, that's exactly what they were!

They conceded their first goal in the third minute, and unfortunately, things only got worse for the sorry Seagulls. By half-time, Norwich were already 10–0 up, and Chadwick had the first of his two hat-tricks in the game. By the final whistle, the score was 18–0, and English league football had a new record victory – or defeat, depending on how you look at it/what side you're on.

Ouch! As the Brighton players trudged off the pitch and began the long journey way back home, had they lost the last of their Christmas cheer? No, not according to Harman: 'I remember afterwards Mr Webb saying how proud he was of us. We knew we didn't have a chance, getting people out of the crowd. Come to think of it, we didn't take it all that seriously, but I'll never forget it.'

After all that bad news, we'll end with some good news for the Seagulls. Wartime matches don't count

as proper Football League fixtures, and so Brighton's worst-ever defeat still officially stands as a 9–0 loss against Middlesbrough in 1958. See, that's only half as bad – much better!

Oh, and in December 1955 (don't worry, way before Christmas this time!), Brighton battered Norwich 6–0 in a Third Division South match that did count. Revenge at last, fifteen years later, for that Christmas Day disaster.

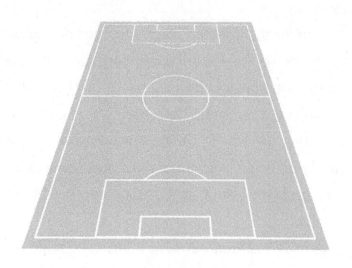

The history of the English Premier League is packed with star-striker partnerships – pairs of attackers who work so well together that it's as if they can read each other's minds:

- Alan Shearer and Chris Sutton at Blackburn Rovers
- Dwight Yorke and Andy Cole at Manchester United
- Dennis Bergkamp and Thierry Henry at Arsenal
- Michael Owen and Emile Heskey at Liverpool
- James Beattie and Marian Pahars at Southampton

    . . . (can you guess what team I support?!)

In 2016–17, a new double act was added to that all-star list:

**Harry Kane and Son Heung-min**

That season, they scored forty-three Premier League goals together, as Tottenham finished second in the table. And the following season, they scored another forty-two, as their team finished third.

Kane was Spurs' main man and top scorer by far, but Son had become a very important and popular player too. On the run, with a football at his feet, he had the speed and skill to dodge past any defenders in his way, as well as the ability to shoot powerfully with both feet. And if that wasn't enough, he also had one of the biggest and best smiles in the game!

In summer 2018, however, Son's winning smile was turned upside down into a frown.

*Oh no, why?* Because the forward was in danger of missing nearly two YEARS of football for Tottenham.

*And again, why?* Because in his home country of South Korea, every man has to do twenty-one months of national service before the age of twenty-eight, even superstar footballers!

In July 2018, Son celebrated his twenty-sixth

birthday, which meant time was really running out for him. Oh dear, what would Tottenham do without him? They had attacking midfielders Christian Eriksen and Dele Alli, wingers Lucas Moura and Erik Lamela, and sub strikers Fernando Llorente and Vincent Janssen. But none of them could score as many goals as Son or link up with Kane in such an exciting way.

### HELP, new superstar needed?

No, not quite yet.

Son still had one last chance to earn a pass. You see, the law in South Korea states that military service applies to all males under the age of twenty-eight, EXCEPT those who:

1. Win an Olympic medal (gold, silver or bronze)
2. Win a gold medal at the Asian Games
3. Have a full-body tattoo!

Well, the next Olympics weren't until 2020, and Son isn't really a full-body-tattoo kind of guy, but the next Asian Games were about to take place in August 2018. A-ha, this was it; now or never.

Winning a trophy for his country was the only way for Son to keep playing for his club. But it wasn't going to be easy. He had been trying, and failing, for years:

- **2011** – In his first international tournament, Son helped South Korea reach the semi-finals of the Asian Cup, where they lost to Japan on penalties

- **2012** – South Korea won the bronze medal at the London Olympics, but Son wasn't there because he stayed at his German club, Hamburg, instead

- **2014** – Son scored at his first World Cup in Brazil, but his team finished bottom of their group

- **2014** – South Korea won the gold medal at the Asian Games, but Son wasn't part of the team because his club, Bayer Leverkusen, wouldn't let him go!

- **2015** – In this Asian Cup, South Korea made it to the final, but despite Son's late equaliser, they ended up losing to Australia in extra-time

- **2016** – At the Summer Olympics in Brazil, 'the Taeguk Warriors' suffered a shock 1–0 defeat to

Honduras in the quarter-finals

- **2018** – At the next World Cup in Russia, they were knocked out in the group stage again

Poor Son! Now, his hopes of avoiding military service rested on South Korea winning the Asian Games. So, in August 2018, while his club teammates kicked off their new Premier League campaign, he set off from London to Indonesia.

'I feel sorry because Tottenham is my team and I feel very sorry to be leaving my teammates,' he said. 'But I am playing for my country and that is also important.'

Son began the tournament on the bench for South Korea, but after a 2–1 loss to Malaysia, he was back in the starting line-up for their crucial last group game against Kyrgyzstan. And what did he do? He fired in the winning goal, of course. Nice one, Son!

In the Round of 16, South Korea beat Iran without any problems, but in the quarter-finals, they really struggled against Uzbekistan. With 20 minutes to go, they were losing 3–2. It was time for their experienced superstars to step up and shine . . .

When a defender slipped, Son pounced straight away and then played a great pass through to Hwang Ui-jo, who finished in style. 3–3!

Then in extra-time, Hwang Ui-jo won a penalty, which South Korea . . . scored – 4–3!

(Son was so nervous he couldn't watch the spot-kick,

so he turned around and faced the other way!)

Phew, the Taeguk Warriors were still on track to win that Asian Games gold medal! Two days later, they beat Thailand 3–1 in the semis to set up a final against their big rivals, Japan. Ooooooh, this was it. Son's best chance yet. Could he lead South Korea to a trophy at last? The whole country crossed their fingers – and so did the Spurs supporters all over the world.

In the fifth minute, he burst forward on the attack and then slid the ball to Hwang In-beom on the right, who crossed it to Hwang Ui-jo at the back post .    . .

But he couldn't quite reach it!

Arghhh, that was the story of the first 90 frustrating minutes for South Korea – lots  of chances created, but no goals scored. When the final whistle blew, it was still 0–0. Time for extra-time!

A penalty shoot-out was looming and the pressure was building, but Son didn't panic. He waited patiently for another chance to arrive, and when it did, he cut inside off the wing, dribbled into the box, and then left the ball for Lee Seung-woo, who slammed a shot into the top corner. 1–0!

Hurray, South Korea had the lead, but they didn't have the trophy yet. They needed another goal to make sure. Minutes later, Son chipped a high free-kick to Hwang Hee-chan (now at Wolves) at the back post, who powered a header down into the bottom corner. 2–0!

Two goals for South Korea, two assists for Son – what a captain's performance in the Asian Games final!

Although Japan pulled one goal back, the Taeguk Warriors held on for the win. When it was all over, Son raced around the pitch, hugging his teammates and crying tears of joy, pride and relief. He had done it; he had successfully led his country to victory!

But even as he celebrated in front of the South Korea fans, holding a national flag in each hand, Son still had his club on his mind. **'Tottenham have supported me so much and that means a lot to me,' he said. 'I really want to say thank you to the coach and the fans of**

**Spurs. They are so special.'**

Everyone at Tottenham breathed a big sigh of relief: **new superstar NOT needed!** Soon, their favourite smiling South Korean was back and starring alongside Kane in attack. That season, Spurs made it all the way to the UEFA Champions League final and Son played a massive part, scoring three goals as they beat Manchester City in the quarters. What on earth would Tottenham have done without him for nearly two years?!

Thanks to that Asian Games gold medal, Son no longer had to do the full twenty-one months of military service in South Korea, but he did still have to do a shorter spell. 'It was a good experience,' he said after. 'The three weeks were tough but I tried to enjoy it.'

Don't worry, Tottenham fans – he did it in June 2020, while the season was still suspended due to COVID-19, so he didn't miss a single match. Now that's what I call a hero, for club AND country.

# The Four Keepers of Comoros

In modern football, there are lots of very talented and useful players who can play in multiple positions:

- **Trent Alexander-Arnold** – right-back/central midfield
- **David Alaba** – left-back, centre-back/left midfield
- **Bernardo Silva** – right wing/left wing/central midfield/attacking midfield/false nine . . .

There is one position on the pitch, however, that stands out from the rest, and is much harder to learn or replace: goalkeeper!

Yes, throwing, catching, punching, saving, diving (OK, some players definitely know how to do that last one!) – goalkeeping is a specialist role that takes years of practice to master. That's why when it comes to game-time, teams always have a back-up keeper on the bench,

and when it comes to competition-time, teams always have at least three keepers in their squad.

Over the course of a two-week tournament, three is usually enough, but sadly not for poor Comoros in this wild story . . .

Before we get on to their goalkeeper crisis, let me tell you a bit about Comoros and their football team. It's a country in Southeast Africa, which is made up of three islands – Anjouan, Moheli and Grande Comore – and sits in the Indian Ocean between Mozambique and Madagascar. The Comoros islands are famous for whale-watching and known as 'the Perfumed Islands' because the plants and trees there make everything smell so good!

And their football team? Well, unlike a lot of African nations, they don't have a fun, catchy nickname, like:

- **'The Indomitable Lions'** (Cameroon)
- **'The Copper Bullets'** (Zambia)
- My personal favourite, **'the National Thunder'** (Equatorial Guinea)

No, instead, the Comoros team is called 'the Coelacanths'. The . . . what? Apparently, it's a type of fish that was thought to be extinct for 70 million years but was rediscovered in 1938 in the waters around the islands. Hmm, when a nickname needs that much explaining, it's never a great sign, is it?

Anyway, from their first game in 1979 until 2005, the Comoros football team was a bit like those coelacanths, only playing in local tournaments, and the rest of the football world hardly knew they existed.

It's not surprising though. Comoros is a small country, and the islands only have a population of 850,000 people, which is about the same as the English city of Liverpool. With so few footballers to choose from, how could they possibly be expected to compete against the bigger African countries, like Nigeria (population 213 million), Egypt (110 million), Ghana (33 million) and Cameroon (27 million)?

Eventually, however, Comoros decided to give it a go. Why not? After all,

anything can happen in football! In 2005, they joined FIFA, in 2007, they entered World Cup qualification, and in 2010, they entered qualification for the Africa Cup of Nations.

The Coelacanths didn't make it to any of the next five of the major African tournaments, but the more matches they played together, the more the team improved. And, in 2019, they finally achieved their aim, winning 1–0 away against Togo and drawing 0–0 with Mo Salah's Egypt to book a place at the 2021 Africa Cup of Nations in Cameroon. Hurray!

As the 133rd best team in the world, Comoros went into the tournament as the third-lowest ranked side, behind Ethiopia (137) and Gambia (147). So, low-to-zero expectations, right? After two narrow defeats against Gabon and Morocco, the Coelacanths seemed to be just playing for pride in their final group game against four-time African champions Ghana. But instead, they battled their way to a 3–2 win, pulling off one of the biggest upsets in the competition's history. And that wasn't all; the surprise victory sent Comoros through to the last 16! So far, so fairy tale.

Now, at last, we get to the goalkeeper crisis part of this story. Like most teams at the Africa Cup of Nations, Comoros had selected three of them in their squad:

1. Salim Ben Boina
2. Moyadh Ousseni
3. Ali Ahamada

During the amazing match against Ghana, Ben Boina had been stretchered off with a shoulder injury, so Comoros were down to only two keepers. Disappointing, but not disastrous, right? But as the team prepared for their 'Last 16' clash with Cameroon, **twelve** of their players tested positive for COVID-19, including both Ousseni AND Ahamada.

Uh-oh, all three keepers down!

Could Comoros delay the match by a few days? No, the tournament rules stated that if a team had eleven fit players, then the game had to go ahead. OK, well there was only one thing for it: one of their outfield players

would just have to go in goal instead, in the biggest match in the country's football history!

But who would it be?

**'HELP, new keeper needed!'**

Some teams might have panicked in their tricky situation, but Comoros kept calm and carried on. 'We are laughing about it,' said their goalkeeping coach, Jean-Daniel Padovani. 'We prefer to approach it this way. It is funny.' OK, if you say so – I'd be terrified!

After testing out a few different players in practice, Comoros picked their new number 1. 'We have already chosen an outfield player who will start as keeper,' Padovani announced.

Who would it be? Rafidine Abdullah, the number 13?

The coach wouldn't say: 'It's a player who in training has shown that he can play as a keeper.'

Hmm, how mysterious! At last, on match day, the team sheet was revealed, and there at the top of the list was . . . Chaker Alhadhur!

Alhadhur usually played at left-back for Comoros,

but not any more; now, he was their new keeper!

So, could he save the day against the tournament hosts Cameroon? Well, before Alhadhur could even get his gloves on the ball, another disaster struck. Yes, this underdog story is about to become a double underdog story. Because not only were Comoros playing without a proper keeper, but in the seventh minute, Jimmy Abdou, their centre-back and captain, flew into a dangerous tackle and was sent off!

**'HELP, new captain ALSO needed!'**

Despite being down to ten players including one (potentially) dodgy keeper, Comoros kept going, and after 25 minutes, the score was still 0–0. Moments later, however, Cameroon took the lead, with their first shot on target. Alhadhur dived down and tried to stop Karl Toko Ekambi's strike, but into the bottom corner it rolled.

Uh-oh, would that goal be the start of a thrashing?

No, the score stayed at 1–0 for ages, largely thanks to the great work of Comoros' new keeper!

It started early in the second half, when Alhadhur

stopped a header from Vincent Aboubakar. Yes, the ball flew straight at him, and yes, he blocked it with his legs like a defender, but hey, a save is a save!

That seemed to give Alhadhur a confidence boost because a few minutes later, he was at it again. First, he threw himself down to punch away a shot from Aboubakar, and then he got straight back up to stop Moumi Ngamaleu's shot too. *DOUBLE SAVE!*

What a hero!

Thanks to their keeper, Comoros were still in the game, but in the 70th minute, Cameroon finally scored again. Aboubakar faked to shoot and left Alhadhur sitting on the grass like a fool, before sliding the ball past him.

Despite all the setbacks they had suffered, Comoros didn't give up. In the 81st minute, they won a free-kick and up stepped midfielder (and former Oldham Athletic player) Youssouf M'Changama to blast a swerving, 30-yard screamer into the top corner.

2–1 – game on? No, unfortunately, Comoros couldn't grab an equalising goal before the final whistle blew, but still, what an incredible effort it had been!

At their first ever major tournament, with no proper available keeper (no offence, Alhadhur!), and with only ten players for nearly 90 minutes, they had only lost 2–1 against Cameroon, one of Africa's top teams!

What an achievement, and Comoros have already proved that first major tournament wasn't a flukey one-off. In November 2023, they beat Ghana again, this time in qualification for the 2026 FIFA World Cup. Who was in goal for the Coelacanths, you ask? Don't worry, Ben Boina was back, back where he belongs!

# WEIRD & WONDERFUL

## The Battle of Bramall Lane

To finish this section on a high, here's an unbelievable football fact for you:

Law 3 of the FA 'Laws of the Game' states that for a game to go ahead, both teams must have a minimum of seven players on the pitch. In the history of English professional football, only one match has ever been abandoned due to a shortage of players. That one match? Sheffield United vs West Bromwich Albion in the First Division (now called 'The EFL Championship'), 16 March 2002.

Or as it's more commonly known, The Battle of Bramall Lane . . .

While West Brom were in third place and focused on trying to win promotion back to the Premier League, Sheffield United were way down in mid-table, with nothing to lose. Except players, apparently.

Let's start the countdown.

As with most matches, it kicked off with **11** but soon it was down to . . .

. . . **10!** In the ninth minute, their goalkeeper Simon Tracey rushed out of his penalty area and blocked a shot with his arms. RED CARD!

It was a disastrous start, but for the next 55 minutes, Sheffield United kept calm and carried on playing football. When West Brom went 2–0 up, however, the Sheffield United manager Neil Warnock decided to make a double substitution, bringing on midfielder Georges Santos and striker Patrick Suffo. And that's when the real battle began . . .

. . . **9!** As Santos ran on to the pitch, he appeared to have only one thing on his mind: revenge. The previous season, he had suffered a nasty eye injury in a bad clash with midfielder Andy Johnson. So as soon as his opportunity arrived, Santos took it. He launched himself – studs up and stamping – into a horror tackle on Johnson. RED CARD!

And with tempers rising, the referee was soon holding up another one . . .

. . . **8!** Like his fellow sub Santos, Suffo seemed to be in a hurry to hurt someone and get sent off. As the two teams argued, the Cameroon striker defended his naughty teammate by headbutting the West Brom captain Derek McInnes, right in front of the ref. RED CARD!

Wow, Sheffield United were a team in real trouble now! Their eight players did their best to battle on (in a football sense, rather than a fighting sense, mostly), but as the minutes ticked by, they were really starting to struggle.

'HELP, new players needed!' – but Sheffield United had already made all three of their substitutions, and so . . .

. . . 7! In the 79th minute, midfielder Michael Brown limped off with an injury.

OK, that was it; Sheffield United really couldn't afford to lose any more players . . .

. . . 6! Then in the 82nd minute, defender Robert Ullathorne had to hobble off too.

Uh-oh, what now? The referee had no choice but to abandon the match right there, with ten minutes of the match still to play.

West Brom were winning 3–0 when the match was stopped, but would they be up for a replay? No way! 'If we are called back to Bramall Lane, we shall kick off and then walk off the pitch,' their angry manager Gary Megson said. 'I've never ever witnessed anything as disgraceful as that.'

In the end, that protest wasn't necessary. West Brom were awarded a 3–0 win and Sheffield United were fined £10,000, with six-game bans for both Santos and Suffo.

So, any regrets? No, strangely, eighteen years later in 2020, Suffo said, 'When I look back at my career and at the highlights, that game is right up there with winning the Olympics and playing in the World Cup.'

Really, Patrick? Whatever you say!

HALF
TIME!

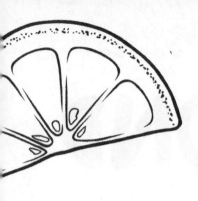

Wow, what an action-packed first 45 minutes, eh?

Grab an orange slice from the team box, glug down some water and take a break.

# SECOND HALF!

That's enough rest for now. There are plenty more unbelievable stories to come!

So let's get going again and sprint into the second half . . .

# CHAPTER FOUR

# RED CARDS AND
# DIRTY FOOTBALL

So far in this book, we've tried to keep the stories funny and feel-good, inspiring and impressive. But what about the nasty stuff that doesn't necessarily have a happy ending: **the fouls, the fights, the dirty football?** Well, fear not (if that's your kind of thing) because it's right here.

# The Clever Couple Who Came Up with Yellow and Red Cards

*'Come on, ref – that's a yellow at least!'*
*'Nah, he's lucky not to get a red for that!'*

These days, the two colours of card are such a central part of football that it feels like they've always been there, but in fact, they're only fifty-eight years old, the same age as England's World Cup win!

The idea of a referee warning and then removing a player from the match for breaking the rules is almost as old as football itself. It was first introduced way back in 1881, but for the next eighty-five years, the act of sending someone off simply involved:

- A few short and loud blasts of the referee's **whistle**
- **Words** – 'Please leave the pitch . . . NOW!'

- A sweeping **wave** of the arm or point towards the touchline
- The referee **writing** down the name of the player in their pocket notebook (that's why we call it a 'booking'!)

Most of the time, that was enough, but when football matches got really fierce and chaotic, especially between teams from different countries, it could all get quite confusing quite quickly. Communication was key on the pitch, but which language to use, and which gesture to make?

Ken Aston from Colchester, England knew all about how difficult life could be as an international referee. At the 1962 World Cup in Chile, he had been in charge of the famously angry group-game between Italy and Chile, later known as 'the Battle of Santiago'.

The fouling started after twelve seconds and by the eighth minute, Aston had seen enough. Pulling his notebook out of his back pocket and then pointing towards the touchline, he sent off Giorgio Ferrini for a blatant kick, but the Italian refused to leave the pitch until policemen dragged him away!

After that, the chaos and confusion continued. Twice, a Chilean player punched an Italian player, but somehow got away with it. Then, when Mario David fought back with an astonishing flying kick, he was sent off! It didn't seem very fair, and it certainly didn't seem like sport. The English TV presenter David Coleman described it as 'the most stupid, appalling, disgusting and disgraceful exhibition of football possibly in the history of the game.'

Poor Aston never refereed a World Cup match again, but it did get him thinking. Surely, there had to be a better way for referees to clearly communicate their decisions on the pitch, to help them keep games calm and under control . . .

Although he didn't referee at the next World Cup in 1966, he was asked to join FIFA's Referees' Committee instead, which meant watching all the matches and helping out with any controversial moments. This time, there was nothing quite as bad as the Battle of Santiago, but England's quarter-final against Argentina did get pretty angry! Again, a player was sent off – Argentina's captain Antonio Rattín – and again, they refused to leave the pitch for ages, later claiming that they hadn't understood what the referee was saying.

After the match, there was also confusion over which of England's Charlton brothers had been booked – Jack, Bobby or both? No one seemed to know the answer – not the players out on the pitch, not the managers on the touchline, not the supporters in the stands, and not the newspapers reporting after the game!

Again, Aston thought to himself, surely there had to be a better way for referees to make things clear . . . What if they used bright colours to create simple signals that everyone could understand, no matter where they were from or what language they spoke? Yes, Aston was on to something . . .

'As I drove down Kensington High Street, the traffic light turned red,' he explained years later. 'I thought, *Yellow, take it easy; red, stop, you're off.*'

A-ha, what a great idea! But how would referees carry and show these colours in a way that everyone could see – players, managers and supporters?

That's where Hilda comes into this story. Ken returned home and told his wife about his idea, and then she had a brainwave too. She disappeared into another room and returned holding two rectangular pieces of card – one yellow, one red. Hilda had cut them down so they were small enough to fit into the front pocket of her husband's refereeing shirt. A-ha! Together, the Astons had just changed football forever.

Ken quickly took their incredible idea to FIFA, who liked it so much that they agreed to trial yellow and red cards at the next World Cup in Mexico. And did the new system work well? Oh yes, everyone agreed that the cards were there to stay, even though they didn't actually get as much use as Aston had expected. The behaviour was much better at the 1970 World Cup, with only five yellows awarded, and zero reds!

Oh well, maybe a player would finally 'see red' at the

next tournament? While the Astons waited for their big moment to arrive, there were plenty more important football problems for Ken to solve, including:

- **The Problem of an Injured/Ill Referee!**

  Aston's answer: appoint a substitute referee for every match

- **The Curse of the Flat Football!**

  Aston's answer: add the perfect ball pressure to the Laws of the Game (in case you wondered, the perfect pressure is: 0.6–1.1 atmosphere (600–1,100g/cm$^2$) at sea level

- **The Mystery of the Hard-to-See Substitutions!**

  Aston's answer: introduce a number board to clearly show the shirt numbers of the players coming on and off the pitch

Wow, they should have called Ken 'the Sherlock Holmes of Football'! But now it's time to return to . . .

**The Case of the Yellow and Red Cards . . .**

On 14 June 1974, the next World Cup finally kicked off, with the hosts West Germany taking on Aston's old trouble-makers Chile. Chile's striker Carlos Caszely had already been booked (and West Germany were already winning), when in the 66th minute, he flew into another angry tackle, this time on defender Berti Vogts.

Ooooooh, was this it – the big moment the Astons had been waiting for?

*'Come on, ref – that's gotta be a red!'*

As Vogts and Caszely both rolled around on the grass, the Turkish referee Doğan Babacan had a chance to make international football history – was he going to take it? With a blast of his whistle and a wave of his arm, the referee called Caszely over and then slowly pulled a card out of his shirt pocket . . .

. . . RED!

'Hurrrraaaaaaaaaaaaaayyyyyy!' roared the home crowd of Germans.

But what about Caszely? Would he refuse to leave the field too? No, instead he just hung his head in shame, turned and trudged off the field.

Thanks to the Astons' clever new card system,

footballers could no longer claim that they didn't understand the referee's decision. The beautiful game was back under control . . . for now.

**FUN FACT:** This wasn't Aston's first football problem-solving mission either – nearly twenty years earlier in 1947, he helped solve another important issue. On dark or foggy days, referees were struggling to see their assistants on the sidelines, so Aston came up with the idea of giving them brightly coloured flags to wave. And the colours he chose? Yellow and red!

The Battle of Santiago in 1962, Carlos Caszely in 1974 – sorry, Chile supporters, but your national team is also at the centre of this next story of unbelievable football nastiness!

With the 1990 World Cup coming up soon in Italy, countries from every continent were competing to qualify. As the reigning champions, Argentina were already through to the tournament, so that left nine South American national teams fighting for just two World Cup places (plus a play-off spot). Let the battle begin!

In Group One, Uruguay finished as winners, beating Bolivia on goal difference. With six points, they were off to Italy!

In Group Two, Colombia were the team on top, but

with only five points, they would have to wait and see what happened in . . .

Group Three! The mighty Brazil were expected to breeze their way to the World Cup as usual, but with one game to go, they were tied at the top with Chile. And the final group match? Brazil versus Chile at the Maracanã Stadium in Rio de Janeiro!

Oooooh, were Brazil, the three-time World Cup winners, in danger of missing the tournament for the first time ever?

When the two teams had met in Chile a month before, it had been more of a war than a football match, with two red cards in the opening 15 minutes. Chile, however, had managed to hold on for a draw, so what would their gameplan be this time?

'La Roja' ('The Reds') were determined to knock their famous football neighbours out of the World Cup. A little too determined, as it turned out . . .

The first half was a 0–0 snooze-fest, so we'll skip straight to the 49th minute. Bebeto threaded a brilliant pass through to Careca, who dribbled into the Chile box and hit a bobbly shot that flicked up off the keeper's left glove and bounced into the net.

***1–0!***

Panic over. Brazil seemed to be on their way to yet another World Cup . . . or were they? All of a sudden, in the 67th minute, the Chile goalkeeper Roberto Rojas fell to the ground in his penalty area, holding his gloved hands to his face. A loud roar went up around the Maracanã and the Chile players quickly alerted the referee. What had just happened?

There was a big cloud of smoke surrounding Rojas – had he been hit by a flare thrown by one of the Brazilian fans behind the goal?

It certainly looked that way. There was a long pause as the Chile team doctors rushed on to the field to treat their injured keeper. Eventually Rojas was carried off the pitch in the arms of his teammates, with his face and shirt covered in blood.

The Chile players were furious, and they walked off

the pitch in protest. There was no way that the game could go on after a violent attack like that! It wasn't safe. Surely, the match should be abandoned, Chile should be awarded the victory, and Brazil should be punished for the bad behaviour of their supporters?

Chile got their wishes; well, the first of them, anyway. After speaking to some important-looking men in suits, the referee waved his arms in the air – the match had been called off!

And what would the consequences be for Brazil – were they in trouble, could they be kicked out of the 1990 World Cup, with Chile taking their place? Not so fast . . . first, the incident had to be properly investigated by CONMEBOL, the South American Football Confederation.

They started by looking for any video evidence of the attack, but unfortunately the TV cameras had missed the crucial moment when the flare landed on the pitch. OK, well what about eye-witnesses? Yes, there were lots of those, but they told a very different version of events:

'We photographers were sitting along the side line and saw the flare come over,' said Paulo Teixeira. 'I was amazed to see Rojas rolling over and bleeding from an eye, as the device had hit the ground about a metre from him.'

Hmmm, that sounded very suspicious indeed, but were there any photos to back up what Teixera had seen? Yes, luckily for Brazil, another photographer called Ricardo Alfieri had managed to take a few shots, which revealed the shocking truth – the flare hadn't hit the Chile keeper at all!

Woah, talk about a full-blown FOOTBALL SCANDAL!

So, what had *really* happened in that crazy moment at

the Maracanã? Why had Rojas fallen to the floor, and where had the blood come from? When CONMEBOL questioned the keeper, it all became clear: he had cut *himself* with a razor blade hidden in his goalie gloves!

What a strange, extreme thing to do, just to try and qualify for the World Cup! And the weirdest part? Rojas actually played his club football for São Paulo, a team in Brazil! Well, he used to, anyway. There was no way they were going to take him back after that.

The Chile keeper was clearly the chief villain, but could he really have pulled off such a nasty trick all on his own, without any of his teammates or coaches knowing? No, it turned out that the manager Orlando Aravena and the team doctor Daniel Rodriguez had both been in on the evil plot too!

**'Chile had a plan which they had prepared and it was unbelievable, truly unbelievable,'** said the stunned Brazil captain Ricardo Gomes. **'The strangest thing is they had a good team.'**

In the end, FIFA awarded Brazil a 2–0 win and

punished Chile's three troublemakers with lifetime bans: Rojas from playing football, and Aravena and Rodriguez from coaching. FIFA also banned the Chile national team from competing at the 1994 World Cup, and which country went on to win the tournament? That's right – Brazil! Chile's evil plan had really backfired.

But after all that talk of dirty tactics, I'd like to end this story on a nicer note. Yes, Rojas committed a major football crime that day at the Maracanã. But he did confess, and everyone makes mistakes, right? He also apologised to the football world, admitting, 'I did it for passion, for Chile to have a chance.'

For the next few years, Rojas was out in the football wilderness, but in 1993, he got a surprise call from his old Brazilian club, São Paulo. All was forgiven; they wanted him to come back and work as their goalkeeping coach! Rojas said yes, and thus began his journey to redemption in Brazil.

His first good deed was training up a young keeper called Rogério Ceni, who went on to become one of São

Paulo's all-time greats, playing 870 games and even scoring 103 goals (mostly penalties and free-kicks!), as well as a member of the Brazil national squad that won the 2002 World Cup.

In 2001, FIFA agreed to lift Rojas' lifetime ban from football, because of his apology and good behaviour. Then two years later, when São Paulo sacked their manager Oswaldo de Oliveira, Rojas was asked to take over for the rest of the season. And what a job he did, leading the club all the way to the Copa Libertadores, South America's biggest club competition, for the first time since 1994.

So, while the main message of this story is, 'Cheating is bad and it never pays!', another would be, 'It's never too late to make up for your mistakes.'

# Zizou Loses His Head

From one big moment of football madness, we're moving on to another, even bigger one. Playing in a World Cup final is a massive achievement for anyone, but for Zinedine Zidane in 2006, it would also be the very last match of his incredible career. France vs Italy at the Olympiastadion in Berlin – the stage was set for 'Zizou' to say goodbye to football in style.

But first, let's rewind and start the story properly, way back in 1998. That year, France were the World Cup hosts and with a winning mix of youth and experience, they made it all the way to the final for the first time ever.

France were a solid team with lots of talented players, but no stand-out superstar . . . so far. That night in Paris, however, that all changed. In the biggest game, against

Brazil – the best team in the world – one player rose high above everyone else: Zidane.

In the 27th minute, he jumped up and powered the ball down into the bottom corner. *GOAL!*

Then just before half-time, Zizou did it again. Another corner, another header. *GOAL!*

France had a new national hero and football had a new superstar. Zidane had always been a beautiful midfield playmaker who glided around the pitch so elegantly, taking perfect touches and playing perfect passes. But in that 1998 World Cup final, he also proved that he was a real big-game player, and there would be plenty more of those to come:

- **Euro 2000** – France made back-to-back major international tournament wins, with Zizou receiving the Player of the Tournament award for his stunning performances.

- **2002 Champions League final** – In 2001, Zidane left Juventus to become Real Madrid's latest Galáctico signing for a world-record fee of

£69.8 million. So, could he live up to his reputation and deliver more major trophies? Oh yes, he could!

With the 2002 Champions League final tied at 1–1, Roberto Carlos flicked a high ball over to Zizou, who swivelled his body and hit the sweetest volley you'll ever see. Not only was it the matchwinner, but it was also one of the greatest-ever Champions League goals. (If you haven't seen it, please stop reading and watch it RIGHT NOW!)

In those magical moments, Zizou looked unstoppable, but after France's awful 2002 World Cup and even more embarrassing Euro 2004, he made a shock announcement – he was retiring from international football, aged just 32!

What? Why?

*Noooooo, please don't go!* the French people begged. But their hero had made up his mind. 'Something is a little bit broken,' he said mysteriously.

Spoiler alert: that's not the end of the story. In fact, we're only really getting to the beginning.

A year and lots of bad results later, Zizou agreed to come back, as France captain, for one final tournament: the 2006 World Cup. This was it; the last dance of one of the game's most graceful movers.

In the group stage, Zizou did little more than pick up two yellow cards and miss the third match, but that didn't matter. Everyone knew he always saved his best performances for the biggest games. Now, it was knock-out time, for France and their captain!

Zidane knew that each match could be his last, and so he played that way, raising his game to the highest level:

### Round of 16, France vs Spain

Against his Real Madrid teammates Iker Casillas, Sergio Ramos and Raúl, Zizou set up France's second goal with a curling free-kick, and then scored the third himself with a cool, calm finish on the counter-attack. Game over!

'I just want to say to the Spanish, it's not yet time for my testimonial,' he joked afterwards. 'The adventure continues.'

### Quarter-finals, France vs Brazil

Zizou wasn't the only football superstar who was retiring after the 2006 World Cup; so was one of his old Real Madrid teammates, the Brazilian striker Ronaldo. Only one of them could make it through to play another match, but who would it be?

Answer: Zidane!

With the pressure on against the reigning world champions, he put on maybe his best-ever midfield masterclass. Every touch was silky, every pass was clever, and every skill was sublime. Brazil tried and tried, but they just couldn't get the ball off him! And then for the big finale – a whipped free-kick to the back post where Thierry Henry was waiting.

*1–0 to France!*

But Zizou wasn't done . . .

### Semi-finals, France vs Portugal

In the semis, he faced another retiring superstar, and former Real Madrid teammate: Luís Figo. Only one of them could make it through, but who would it be?

Answer: Zidane, and he even scored France's winner from the penalty spot!

It was meant to be. Even William Shakespeare couldn't have written a more perfect ending. Zizou's last game as a professional footballer would be the biggest game of all . . .

### The 2006 World Cup final, France vs Italy

When the big game in Berlin kicked off, it seemed like it was going to be 1998 all over again. France were awarded an early penalty and up stepped their captain to score in the most Zizou way possible: a glorious 'Panenka' chip down the middle of the goal, which kissed the underside of the crossbar and bounced over the line.

*1–0 to France!*

**'IN HIS HEAD, THE PLAN WAS CLEAR: ZIDANE WOULD RETIRE AFTER WINNING THE WORLD CUP FOR A SECOND TIME'**

– Matthew Spiro

Italy, however, had other ideas, especially their centre-back Marco Materazzi. He equalised with a towering header to take the final to extra-time.

Come on, Zizou! Could France's captain come up with one more big World Cup moment?

Yes, but it wasn't what the fans were hoping for . . .

In the 99th minute, he ghosted into the box, unmarked, to meet a cross from Willy Sagnol. *This is it; our winning goal!* the France fans thought excitedly. But his header flew straight at Gianluigi Buffon.

Nooo, what a brilliant chance wasted!

By then, Zizou was feeling seriously tired and seriously fed up. This wasn't how his grand football finale was supposed to go! Materazzi could sense his opponent's frustration, and he knew that beneath the calm surface, the France captain had a hot temper.

As a younger player at Bordeaux and Juventus, anger had been Zidane's biggest weakness, and he had also been sent off at the 1998 World Cup for a stamp on Saudi Arabia defender Fuad Anwar.

Hmm, maybe, with a few nasty words, Materazzi could make Zizou lose his head again? He was a pretty dirty defender who would do anything to win a match, let alone a World Cup, and so he decided to have a go at winding the great man up. Unfortunately for Zizou, it worked . . .

As he jogged back towards the halfway line, Zidane suddenly turned around and pushed his head into Materazzi's chest with the power he usually put into heading the ball.

What? Why? Noooooo, Zizou!

It was a shocking moment of madness, and although the referee didn't see it, the linesman did.

**RED CARD!**

Zidane had been sent off in the World

Cup final, and his final match as a professional footballer. Head down, he walked slowly off the pitch for the last time, past the World Cup trophy that he was supposed to win for a second time, and down the tunnel. What a wild and dramatic way to say goodbye!

France managed to hold on for penalties, but without their first-choice taker, they lost the shoot-out. Italy were the new World Champions, and France had no one to blame but Zizou.

'I want to ask for forgiveness from all the children who watched that,' he said in a TV interview a few days later. 'There was no excuse for it.'

So, would the country accept Zizou's apology?

Just four days after the World Cup final, data showed that 61 per cent of French people had already forgiven Zidane for his headbutt. In fact, many supporters seemed to love him more than ever. By doing something so stupid in such a massive match, he had shown that, despite his out-of-this-world football skills, he was human, after all. Zizou sometimes made mistakes, just like everyone else. Not very many, though. Overall, Zidane's success rate was remarkable as a player, and it's been even better since he became a boss. As Real Madrid manager from 2016 to 2018, he helped the club win the UEFA Champions League three times in three years. And he didn't get sent off at all!

# The Three Yellow Cards of Josip Šimunić

They say cats have nine lives, and footballers? Well, they're supposed to only get two yellow cards before they're sent off. But at the 2006 World Cup, one lucky player was given a third chance . . .

In the final game of Group F, Croatia and Australia were competing for the chance to finish second behind Brazil. A draw would send Australia through, but if Croatia won, they would qualify for the Round of 16 instead.

It was a big game for every player on the pitch, but especially for Josip Šimunić. Although the centre-back was representing Croatia, he was actually born and grew up in Australia. And that wasn't the only weird and wonderful fact that would come out of this match . . .

With Croatia winning 2–1 in the second half, Šimunić was determined to protect their lead, even if that meant doing some pretty dirty defending! In the 61st minute, he stopped Harry Kewell's run with a strong arm to the face, and English referee Graham Poll reached straight into his shirt pocket.

**Yellow card number one!**

Kewell could not be stopped for long, though. Eighteen minutes later, the Australian forward fired in to make it 2–2.

Uh-oh, Croatia now needed to score again, otherwise they would be heading home early. With time, energy and patience running out, Šimunić battled for the ball on the halfway line, and ended up wrestling Mark Viduka to the ground, followed by one of his Australia teammates as well.

**Yellow card number two!**

If only Poll had been keeping count. But no, instead of following up with a red card, he got Šimunić confused with someone else, thinking he was the Australia number 3, rather than the Croatia number 3!

But rather than being good and grateful for his surprise third chance, Šimunić decided to keep pushing his luck. After the final whistle, he raced over to the referee for an angry argument. Poll tried to push him away, but the Croatian defender wouldn't budge, so there was only thing for it:

**Yellow card number three, and . . . a red card!**

At last! Come on, Josip – you can't say you didn't get enough chances to behave yourself!

His red card didn't really matter anyway because Croatia were already out of the World Cup. As usual in football, it was the poor match official who suffered the most. While Šimunić went on to play at Euro 2008, Poll never refereed an international game again.

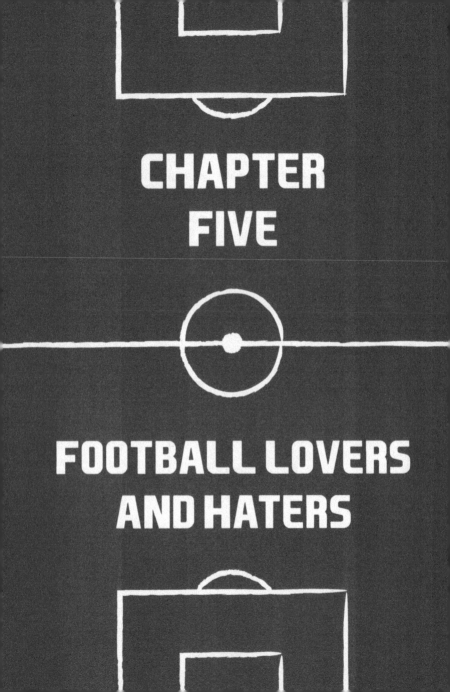

# CHAPTER FIVE

# FOOTBALL LOVERS AND HATERS

Warning! What I'm about to say may cause your head to explode, but here goes:

NOT **EVERYONE** LOVES FOOTBALL . . .

There, I said it – shocking, right? Unbelievable, you might even say. But it's true, and there are some people who even **HATE** it.

*BOOM!* Whoops, there goes your head . . .

In this section, we're going to take a look at both ends of the emotional scale – from football haters to ultimate football mega-fans who maybe love it a bit too much.

Keep calm and carry on reading because there are plenty more shocks to come . . .

When you hear the name 'Adolf Hitler', I'm sure football isn't the first thing you think of. Adolf Hitler was the leader of the Nazi party in Germany and became a powerful dictator (known as the *Führer*), between 1933 and 1945. Hitler and the Nazi party were responsible for many sad and terrible events. He started the Second World War by invading Poland in 1939 and continued to invade other countries across Europe. He was also responsible for some of the most horrible crimes committed in human history, including the murder of more than six million Jews in the Holocaust. There is now a Remembrance Day every year on 27 January remembering the Jewish people and others who the Nazis killed and persecuted. Hitler didn't exercise and he didn't like sports, especially football. According to sports writer Mickaël Correia, 'Hitler detested football, seeing it as too urban and not German enough.'

Despite hating the game himself, Hitler could see that lots of other people loved football, and so he decided it was important for Germany to have a successful national team. That way, he could use the game's popularity to gain more support for his political party, while showing off his country's power to the rest of the world.

That was Hitler's plan, but I'm happy to say that, for the most part, it backfired spectacularly. Instead of bringing pride and joy to Nazi Germany, football caused pain and embarrassment on three famous occasions.

The first moment came in August 1936, during the Olympic Games in Berlin. The big event was supposed to be a celebration of Germany's strength across all sports, and they started well in the football tournament, with a 9–0 thrashing of Luxembourg.

Next up, in the quarter-finals, they faced Norway, who had just beaten

Turkey 4–0. That should have been a warning, but no, Germany were feeling confident. So confident that Nazi officials urged Hitler to come along and watch the game live at the *Poststadion*. Football? Eurgh! But reluctantly, he agreed and took his seat in the official box.

Can you guess what happened next? Yes, instead of storming to an easy victory as expected, Germany lost, in front of 100,000 fans! They went 1–0 down after just seven minutes, thanks to a strike from Magnar Isaksen, and he scored again late in the second half to secure the shock win. Wow, Germany had been knocked out of their own Olympic Games!

So, did their leader accept defeat like a good loser? What do you think?! 'Wild with rage and without waiting for the final whistle, the Führer hastily left the stadium,' Correia writes.

Hurray!

That turned out to be the first and last match he ever attended, but Hitler continued to try and use the game as a political tool.

In 1938, Germany invaded and took over their neighbour Austria (which was also the country where Hitler was born), calling it an *'Anschluss'*, meaning 'connection'. And what better way to celebrate the happy *'Anschluss'* than by holding a friendly football match between the two national teams? The game was to be so friendly that they even agreed what the scoreline would be in advance: 0–0, to symbolise unity and sporting equality.

Booooooooooo – boring! For most of the match, the Austrians played along, but after 77 minutes of trying *not* to score, two of their players couldn't take it any more. Matthias Sindelar was one of the best forwards in Europe, so skilful that they called him 'the Mozart of Football', while Karl Sesta was a talented defender. Together, they were the leaders of Austria's successful *'Wunderteam'*, and they were here to win, not to draw; to play football, not politics.

All of a sudden, Sindelar raced forward on the attack, and after weaving through the German defence, he couldn't help himself. He did what he did best: score. *1–0 to Austria!*

And that wasn't all. Sindelar celebrated his goal by punching the air and doing a little victory dance with Sesta, who then lobbed the keeper from near the halfway line before the final whistle blew. So, it finished:

Austria 2 Germany 0

Hurraaaaay again, but also oooooh, because surely Austria's heroes were in big trouble now? What would the Nazis decide to do with them?

The answer was . . . try to force them to play for Germany instead! Sesta eventually agreed and played three games in 1941, but Sindelar refused, saying that he suddenly had a dodgy knee.

A year after the *Anschluss* with Austria, Hitler invaded

Poland, pushing the British Prime Minister Neville Chamberlain to declare war on Germany and begin the Second World War.

Hitler, however, refused to be stopped. In 1940, he marched German troops into Norway, and then into Belgium, Luxembourg, the Netherlands and France. Then in 1941, he launched 'Operation Barbarossa', an invasion of the Soviet Union (USSR), a communist country that was later divided into fifteen separate countries in 1991, including Russia, Belarus, Kazakhstan and Ukraine.

In Ukraine, all sport stopped once the fighting began, but when the Nazis started their own football championship, a local football fan called Josef Kordik had a brave and brilliant idea. He already had one former player from his favourite team, Dynamo Kyiv, working in his bakery – what if he could get the whole Dynamo team back together to defeat the Nazis on the football pitch?

Eventually, Kordik managed to find eleven players

– seven from Dynamo, and four from their local rivals Lokomotiv Kyiv – to form a new team: FC Start. And once they did start, they couldn't stop winning. They smashed one German team 7–1, thrashed another 9–1, and then beat their best *Luftwaffe* pilots 5–1!

How humiliating to lose like that to a team of hungry local bakers! The Nazis were furious and they demanded a rematch. FC Start agreed, and despite lots of fouling, cheating and even half-time threats, they managed to defeat the German pilots again! It finished:

**FC Start 5 Luftwaffe 3**

Sadly, however, their brave and brilliant victory came at a tragic cost. Afterwards, all of the FC Start players were arrested, some were tortured and some lost their lives.

Not even the beautiful game was powerful enough to stop the rise of the Nazis and the Second World War, but with its popularity and influence, football did provide an effective way for people to come together, to protest against the regime and inflict some humiliating defeats on Hitler.

# The Footballer Who Stole The Scream

Even professional footballers aren't always die-hard football fans. There are some players like Arsenal's Ben White who never actually watches the game, he just likes to play it. While others prefer to do something different when they get a bit of spare time, like:

- Playing golf (Gareth Bale)
- Fishing (Phil Foden and Georgia Stanway)
- Playing musical instruments (goalkeepers Petr Cech – drums – and Alisson Becker – guitar)
- Picking mushrooms (Xavi Hernández)!

But the footballer with the strangest second passion has to be a Norwegian player called Pål Enger. Pål grew up in a poor part of his country's capital city, Oslo, in the 1980s, where life was tough, especially for young people. Many ended up stealing things to earn extra

money, but at first, Pål was determined to follow a different path: getting really good at sport.

Enger dedicated himself fully to football, practising so hard that he was signed up by Vålerenga, Oslo's most successful football team. A skilful midfielder, he was seen as a future star, and at the age of only 19, he was picked to play for his club in the UEFA Cup (now the Europa League).

How exciting! At that moment, Enger seemed to have it all: talent, money, fame and a successful sports career ahead of him. So far, so football fairy tale, but unfortunately, this is where the story takes a dark turn. Because as Enger puts it: **'By day, I was a professional footballer at the best club in Norway. By night, I was the best criminal in Norway.'**

Yes, young Pål wanted to play other, more dangerous and illegal games. So, together with his best friend Bjørn, he began stealing things: jewellery, money from cash machines, cars . . .

Enger soon became a master thief. But the more

time went on, the more ambitious he became. What if he could pull off something really huge, like stealing one of his country's most precious objects?

The precious object that Enger picked was *The Scream* – Norway's most famous and valuable piece of art. Made by Edvard Munch in 1893, the painting hung proudly in the National Gallery in Oslo, where thousands of people came to admire it every year, including Enger himself. He had been obsessed with the artwork for years, ever since he first saw it on a school trip. Now, aged twenty, he had made up his mind – he was going to steal it!

Enger visited *The Scream* at the gallery and counted the windows and pillars to work out where he would need to place the ladder outside to break in and grab it.

There was just one problem: he got his numbers wrong and ended up stealing the wrong painting!

Noooooo. Pål and Bjørn had taken one of Munch's other famous pieces, *Love and Pain* (also called *The Vampire*). What would they do now? They couldn't try to sell it because the theft was all over the news!

For a while, they hid the artwork in the ceiling above the snooker hall they owned. But they couldn't just keep it there forever. The police were still looking for the painting, and besides, it wasn't the one Enger wanted anyway. So eventually, he decided to walk into the local station and hand himself in, along with *Love and Pain.*

*Pål, what on earth were you thinking?!* his teammates wondered in disbelief. He had just thrown away his chance to be Vålerenga's next big thing, and his entire football career was under threat. For what? An old painting that he'd ended up giving back!

Enger was sentenced to four years in prison, which meant that he would be 25 by the time he got out. If he worked really hard, he could perhaps still get back to playing professional football in the lower leagues.

But while he sat in jail, it was announced that the Norwegian town of Lillehammer had been chosen to host the 1994 Winter Olympics. Hurray! It was a really big deal for the country, bringing in lots of tourists and money. But Enger wasn't thinking about any of that.

All he was thinking was, *Once the Olympics start in Lillehammer, there'll be hardly any police left in Oslo – that's the perfect time to steal* The Scream*!*

So rather than getting fit and practising his football skills, Enger spent his years in prison learning everything he could about pulling off the perfect crime.

Then, as soon as he was released, Enger began visiting the National Gallery again, to start planning for the big day: 12 February 1994 – the Olympic opening ceremony. It would be way too obvious if he and Bjørn stole the painting themselves, so Pål found new friends to do it for him. In the end, the theft turned out to be easy to organise because:

1. The gallery only had a few blurry CCTV cameras
2. There was no bulletproof glass
3. They had moved *The Scream* into the main entrance hall for a special Olympic exhibition!

It was all so straightforward that Pål gave his friends a handwritten postcard to leave at the crime scene, which read, '*A thousand thanks for the bad security*'.

When the news was announced, it shocked not just the country, but the whole world – *The Scream*, Norway's most famous piece of art, had been stolen!

The staff at the National Gallery were frantic with worry because Munch had done the painting on cardboard, rather than canvas, which meant it was even more fragile than most old artworks.

*Who would steal such a valuable object, and why, and where was it now?* The Norwegian police suspected Enger straight away, but they couldn't arrest him because they didn't have any proof.

So, now that he finally had it, what was Pål going to do with the painting? Well, nothing of much use. He just kept on playing his games:

1. He made prank phone calls, claiming to have found the painting
2. He did a newspaper interview where he went into the National Gallery and posed for a photo next to the empty wall where *The Scream* was supposed to be

3. He put an advert in the newspaper, announcing that his baby son had just been born 'with a scream'!

As the Norwegian police grew more and more frustrated, they started putting extra pressure on Enger. They followed him everywhere, and even got aggressive with his family and his criminal friends.

Suddenly, Enger wasn't having so much fun any more. He decided it was time to give the painting back and move on, but how could he do it without handing himself in to the police again? The only answer was to find a dodgy art dealer who would just take it away, no questions asked.

So, when a man from the Getty Museum in the USA contacted him, asking to take *The Scream* and put it on display, Enger was seriously interested. It seemed like the perfect way out.

That American gallery owner, however, turned out to be Charley Hill, an undercover officer working for the English police. So, when Enger gave him the painting,

Hill just handed it straight back to the National Gallery in Oslo. Hurray, *The Scream* had been returned, and amazingly, it was hardly damaged at all!

That wasn't the end of this story, though; especially not for Enger. He was arrested, and although he pleaded 'not guilty', the truth was eventually revealed, after a slip-up from his best friend Bjørn. In 1996, Pål was sentenced to six years and three months in prison, Norway's longest-ever sentence for theft.

Enger would be thirty-five by the time he got out – that was too old to go back to being a professional footballer. His sporting days were done, and for what? Some stolen paintings he gave back and years of his life in prison. Lesson: always focus on football . . . and never steal! *The Scream* now hangs safely on the walls of the new National Museum of Norway, which was opened in Oslo in 2022, with – I'm guessing and hoping – a much better security system.

Right, that's enough football-bashing for one book. Now, it's time to take a look at the other end of the emotional scale, and the stories of four fans who love the game A LOT. A little too much, some might say, but I'll leave you to make up your own mind about that . . .

Our first contestant is **Arjan Wijngaard** from the Netherlands. And what makes him such a football mega-fan? Well, how about his incredible collection of more than three thousand football shirts? Yes, you read that right – three thousand! That's nearly twice as many shirts as there are professional clubs in UEFA (the Union of European Football Associations)!

It all started in 1997, when Arjan was given his very first football kit, and you'll never guess what it was.

No, it wasn't the Dutch national team shirt . . . nor

his now-favourite local club FC Groningen . . . nor that year's European Champions, Borussia Dortmund. Give up? Believe it or not, it was . . . an Everton shirt!

And from that bizarre beginning, Wijngaard's collection just grew and grew, until, eventually, he ran out of space in his wardrobe. So, what next – stop buying shirts, sell a few to make some extra room? Nope! Instead, he just rearranged his house to give his football collection a whole room of its own!

Wijngaard also created a website called 'Voetbal Shirts' (*'Voetbal'* is Dutch for 'football'), where the world can look at, and learn about, each and every one of his shirts. What team and season they're from, what size they are, which sports company made them . . . even the name and capacity of the team's stadium!

Don't expect to see many PSG or Manchester City shirts in there, though. 'In general, I like to collect shirts from clubs that are not very easy to find,' says Arjan. 'Like lower and non-league, for example, steps nine and ten of the English pyramid or clubs from countries not

known as famous football countries, like New Zealand or Tanzania.' And that, Arjan Wijngaard, is why you've been selected as our first **ULTIMATE FOOTBALL MEGA-FAN!**

OK, on to contestant number two . . . Rodrigo Romero Saldivar from Mexico. Like Arjan, Rodrigo is also a keen collector but instead of shirts, he's gone for something bigger, rounder and bouncier. Yes, footballs!

While studying in Spain in 2006, Rodrigo took an inspiring trip to the World Cup in Germany, and there he bought his first ball to have a kickaround with his friends. Once he started buying them, however, he found he couldn't stop. By 2020, he had 1,230 of them at his home in Pueblo, earning him the Guinness World Record for the largest collection of footballs.

But before you start panicking about the 'where?!' and the 'how?!', I should explain: Rodrigo's particular passion is *mini* footballs (we're talking mostly sizes 1–3, rather than 5). I mean, can you imagine trying to store more than 1,200 full-size footballs in your house?

Want to hear about Rodrigo's two favourite footballs?

Of course you do! The first is the one his wife, María Jose, gave him to announce that they were having a baby in 2019. Awwww! And the second? A ball he bought at the 2012 Olympic Games in London, where the Mexico national football team won the gold medal, their greatest-ever achievement.

I suppose the other question that might be worth

asking the proud owner of more than 1,200 footballs is 'why?', and here's the answer: 'I want to show them that everything can be achieved if you set your mind to it.'

Bravo, Rodrigo – spoken like a true . . . **ULTIMATE FOOTBALL MEGA-FAN!**

Next up, we have contestant number three . . . **Maria Petri** from England. This time, it's her actions and words, rather than objects, that earn her a place on this very special list.

Born in London in 1939, Maria began watching Arsenal aged 12. Back then, she used to sneak out of the house and into the stadium because her parents didn't want her going to football matches – but she wasn't going to let anything, or anyone, stop her.

Soon, Maria was going to every home game at Highbury, as well as cheering on the club's reserves and youth teams. And in 1987, when Arsenal Ladies were formed, she started going along to watch all of their games too. Yes, that's what I call an . . . **ULTIMATE FOOTBALL MEGA-FAN!**

'Arsenal are my family,' Maria often said, and everyone at the club loved her right back. When Arsenal Women won trophies, the players celebrated with her; when she was stuck at home alone during the COVID-19 lockdown, former player Ray Parlour visited her, and took the FA Cup trophy with him; and when Maria's 'Meado!' chant went viral during UEFA Women's Euro 2022, Beth Mead stopped by to sing it with her.

Maria sadly died in 2022, at the age of 84, after supporting Arsenal for 72 years. And, as you can imagine, the tears and tributes poured out.

'Thank you for the love, the passion, the songs and support for us @ArsenalWFC from the very beginning,' wrote former player Alex Scott. 'We will never forget you Maria. We love you.'

Finally, last but by no means least, is contestant number four . . . **Ali Demirkaya** from Turkey. We should begin this tale with a warning: do NOT try this at your football club . . .

Ali is a die-hard fan of his local team, Denizlispor, but

in April 2018, he was banned from entering their Denizli Atatürk stadium (don't ask me why – the details are a little unclear. . .). With Denizlispor's next home game against Gaziantepspor fast approaching, what was Ali going to do?

A-ha, he had an idea, an idea so unbelievable that only an **ULTIMATE FOOTBALL MEGA-FAN** could possibly have come up with it: he would hire a crane, park it just outside the stadium, raise the bucket as high as it would go . . . and then watch the game from there!

I told you it was unbelievable, but when an ultimate football mega-fan wants to watch their favourite team play, nothing is going to stop them. And guess what? The plan worked! With Ali cheering them on from up above, Denizlispor went on to win 5–0.

So, there you have it – you've met the four finalists, but there can only be one winner. Who will it be? YOU decide! It's time to vote for your . . . **ULTIMATE FOOTBALL MEGA-FAN!**

# The Bad Losers Who Tried to Spoil the Party

From the football lovers to the haters, and now to the sore losers . . .

Losing a football match is never a nice feeling, but losing in front of your own fans, against your biggest rivals, and handing them the league title? Oof, that's really gotta hurt!

Still, I'm guessing most teams in that position would be sporting enough to at least shake their opponents' hands afterwards, and maybe even mumble a very quick, quiet, 'Well done'. When it happened to Alianza Lima in November 2023, however, the club had other, much darker ideas . . .

The night had begun positively for the team from Peru, South America. After finishing the league season in first place, they were now 90 minutes and one win away from being crowned national champions for the third year in a row. And after drawing 1–1 away at Universitario in the first leg of the Liga 1 final, Alianza also now had home advantage. Perfect, what could possibly go wrong? Well, lots of things, actually . . .

In only the third minute of the match, Universitario stunned the Estadio Alejandro Villanueva by taking a shock early lead, and Alianza never really recovered. While it was still 1–0, they were still in the game, but when Horacio Calcaterra made it 2–0 with a stunning late strike? It was game over and league title lost.

Booooooooooooooo! The Alianza fans were furious and so, it seems, were the club's owners. Because just as the final whistle blew and the Universitario players started to celebrate their victory, POOF! Suddenly, the lights went out and the stadium was plunged into darkness!

Liga 1 later claimed that due to a 'power outage', the post-match presentation ceremony was postponed. But the timing was certainly suspicious, and so was the fact the electronic advertising boards around the edge of the pitch stayed on . . .

Cutting the power just to spoil your rivals' party? Ha, how petty. Alianza – you should be ashamed of yourselves! But while no one likes a bad loser, Universitario weren't going to allow anything to ruin their big night. It was the club's first title in ten years, so they focused on the bright side of the situation.

No light? No problem. And the players just danced on in the dark!

No post-match presentation ceremony? No problem. They would just wait and hold that back at their own stadium, packed full of their own fans!

But what about Alianza's bad behaviour – did Universitario just let it go? No, the next day, the club posted a funny social media advert for . . . anti-blackout light-bulbs! Oh and they also managed to mention they'd now won the league twenty-seven times. Yes, two can play that petty game!

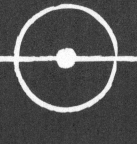

# CHAPTER SIX

# A GAME FOR EVERYONE

So, it's true that not everyone loves football with a fierce passion. But **A LOT** of people do. It's by far the world's most popular sport – look:

3. Basketball – 2.4 billion fans around the world

2. Cricket – 2.5 billion fans

**1. FOOTBALL – 3.5 billion and rising!**

The world's total population is roughly 7.88 billion, so that means nearly half of ALL people are football fans. In 2022, more than 1.5 billion people tuned in to watch one single match: the World Cup final between Argentina and France! And what a great game that turned out to be: Lionel Messi vs Kylian Mbappé, six goals, extra-time *and* penalties.

So, why is football sooooooo popular? Well, along with being really exciting and packed with super-skilful players, the beautiful game is also nice and simple, making it easy for people to get involved.

- **It can be played anywhere** – inside or outside; on concrete, grass or a sandy beach. People have even played football at the North Pole, and they reckon we could be playing on the Moon by 2035!

- **You hardly need any equipment** – sure, having a proper ball helps, but even rolled-up socks will do. Then it's jumpers for goalposts, and off you go!

- **And anyone can play it** – whatever your age, gender, sexuality, religion, wealth, location and ability, there's now a type of football out there for you. Whether it's beach football, street football, walking football, wheelchair football, blind football . . . or even bubble football.

Yes, modern football is a game for everyone. But it wasn't always that way. As you're about to find out, it started off as a game played mostly by the rich . . .

These days, when we talk about 'the elite' of English football, we mean the Premier League Top Six: Manchester City, Manchester United, Liverpool, Arsenal, Tottenham and Chelsea. But in the early years, it was the elite of society who ruled the game: the British Army, top universities and big, expensive private schools.

Charles W. Alcock, the man who came up with the idea of the FA Cup in 1871, is a classic example. After attending Harrow School, one of England's most prestigious private schools, he played for Wanderers Football Club, a team made up mostly of former Harrow students. They went on to win the FA Cup five times in the first eight years. And the other winners?

- Oxford University in 1874
- Royal Engineers (part of the Army) in 1875

- Old Etonians (former pupils from Eton College, another prestigious, expensive school) in 1879

But while wealthy men from the South were dominating English football, they weren't the only ones playing. It was fast becoming 'the people's game', a form of fun exercise for everyone – from business owners to factory workers. So, where were the successful teams from different backgrounds and different parts of the country? Don't worry, they were on their way!

In 1882, Blackburn Rovers, a team from Lancashire in North West England, reached the FA Cup final, where they faced the famous Old Etonians. On that occasion, the 'Old Boys' from the South lifted the trophy again. But the English football revolution had started and the elite's golden era was about to end.

The next year, inspired by Rovers (their local rivals), Blackburn Olympic decided to give the FA Cup their best shot. Most of the team worked in the town's cotton mills, where their bosses had discovered that letting them play football was a brilliant way to stop them from complaining about the poor pay and bad working conditions. If the team went all the way and won the FA Cup, just think what happy workforces they would have!

Olympic decided to boost their chances by bringing in Jack Hunter, a former England international, to be both their new player and manager. They couldn't give him massive wages, though, like modern clubs do. In the 1880s, football was still an amateur sport, which meant players weren't allowed to earn any money from the game. So Olympic said they were paying him to run a pub instead!

Hunter was a man from Yorkshire with very modern football ideas. He didn't want his team to play the old-school, 'Old Boy' 'dribbling game', where players just took it in turns to kick the ball and run. He wanted his players to . . . PASS the ball to each other! Quick, short passes to move the ball up the pitch, as well as long, diagonal passes, from wing to wing. Woah, what a magnificent idea!

Playing their new 'passing game', Olympic flew through the early rounds of the FA Cup:

*6–3 vs Accrington*

*8–1 vs Lower Darwen*

*8–0 vs Darwen Ramblers*

*2–0 vs Church*

*4–1 vs Ruabon Druids . . .*

Olympic were through to the semi-finals, where they faced Old Carthusians, former pupils from Charterhouse School, another prestigious and expensive private school. And how did Hunter's team get on? The Lancashire lads won 4–0! Hurray, Olympic would be playing in the FA Cup final, against . . . Old Etonians.

Oooooooh, what an exciting clash! North versus South, factory workers versus wealthy businessmen, the new passing game versus the old dribbling game – who would be victorious?

As the big game approached, the teams prepared in very different ways. Old Etonians never trained, not (apparently) because they were really lazy, but because

they were a proudly amateur team, who played for fun. Practising before a game was far too professional!

Olympic's players, on the other hand, travelled from Blackburn to London two days early so that they were fit and fresh, and they were even put on a special pre-game diet: 'At 6 a.m., two raw eggs and a glass of port [a type of really strong wine]. Later, after a brisk walk along the sea front, porridge and haddock. For lunch, plates of mutton [like lamb, but from a slightly older sheep], then at teatime more porridge and a pint of milk each. In the evening, half a dozen oysters per man.' Wow, what a menu – something tells me that's not what Pep Guardiola gives his players at Manchester City these days!

Right, let's get to the main event: the 1883 FA Cup final! When the match kicked off at the Kennington Oval, it was Old Etonians who scored first, through one of their five forwards, Harry Goodhart (yes, in those days, 2-3-5 was the most popular formation!).

Noooo, it was a big setback for Olympic, but could

they turn things around? Yes!

Alfred Matthews equalised in the second half, setting up an exciting finale. Which team would grab the FA Cup-winning goal?

Whether it was down to the special diet or the fact that they actually did some training, it's hard to say, but the Olympic players were much fitter than their 'Old Boy' opponents. The longer the match went on, the more the Lancashire lads dominated with their patient, passing game.

Moving the ball from side to side, instead of just booting it forward as quickly as possible?

No, thank you! As sportswriter Conor Pope says, 'The Old Etonians looked down on passing as ungentlemanly and against the spirit of the game.'

When the final whistle blew, the score was still 1–1. What now – shake hands and return a few days later for a replay? No, the Old Etonians didn't think it was fair to ask Olympic to travel all the way from Blackburn again,

so their captain Arthur Kinnaird suggested they play on for another 30 minutes of extra-time!

It was very kind of the Old Etonians to offer, but with members of their team either really tired or really injured, it wasn't very clever. In the 107th minute, Jimmy Costley finally scored for Olympic, and it came from a long diagonal pass from Tommy Dewhurst.

Hurray, Hunter's passing game had worked; Blackburn Olympic had won the FA Cup!

A few days later, the *Morning Post* newspaper summed up the final perfectly in their match report: 'It was a grandly contested trial, and the Blackburn men won by fast play and good condition.' In other, more-modern words, Olympic were fitter and – no offence, Old Etonians – better at football.

When the winning players arrived back in Blackburn, they were welcomed home by a big crowd, and even a brass band. They toured the streets of the town to show off the trophy, but instead of an open-top bus, they travelled in a wagon pulled by horses!

Not everyone was impressed, though. Apparently, one local said, 'Is that the Cup? It looks more like a tea kettle!' Luckily, Albert Warburton, the captain, had a great comeback: 'It might well do to you, but it's welcome here in Lancashire, and it'll never go back to London.'

In the end, Warburton's wish didn't come true, but the trophy did stay in Lancashire for a while longer. Although Olympic couldn't repeat their success, their local rivals, Blackburn Rovers, won it for the next three years in a row.

The 1883 FA Cup final had changed the English game forever. The 'Old Boys' were old news. It was all about the Northern teams now, with their new training and tactics! A few years later, English football took another big step forward. Clubs like Olympic were finally allowed to pay their players, which meant an exciting new professional era had begun. Football was no longer a game designed for wealthy amateurs; it was becoming a game for everyone.

Football: a game for everyone – really? For this next story, we're staying in the English county of Lancashire, but moving from the men's game to the women's game – from the 1880s to the 1950s, and from Blackburn Olympic to the Manchester Corinthians.

But first, a bit of background: during the First World War (1914–18), women's football had become one of the most popular forms of entertainment in England. With the men away fighting for their country, the women had stepped up to take their place, both working in the factories and playing on the football pitches. And could they kick it? Yes, they could, and the Lancashire clubs led the way. Lancaster, Bolton, British Westinghouse and Heywood Ladies were all strong, but Preston's Dick, Kerr Ladies were the best by far. They even called themselves 'world champions' after beating teams from Scotland, Ireland, France, Italy and the USA!

In 1921, however, the good times came to a very sudden and sad end. With the war over and the soldiers back, football returned to being a game that only men played, and according to the Football Association (FA), was seen as 'quite unsuitable for females'. What?! On Boxing Day 1920, Dick, Kerr Ladies had played in front of 53,000 fans at Everton's Goodison Park stadium, but now women's football matches were no longer allowed to take place at FA grounds.

So, was that it – the end for women's football?

No, of course not! They weren't giving up; football was a game for everyone, not just men. The most determined and dedicated females carried on, but with no access to proper pitches in England, they had to find new places to play. In 1926, Dick, Kerr Ladies started again under the new name of Preston Ladies F.C., and after the Second World War (1939–45), more women's football teams followed . . .

**Manchester Corinthians** was formed in 1949 by Percy Ashley, who worked as a scout for Bolton Wanderers and as a local referee. His daughter, Doris, was a very talented footballer but she was deaf, and so Ashley set the club up as a comfortable place for her to play sport and make friends.

Comfortable, however, is not a word you'd use to describe the place Corinthians called 'home'. At Fog Lane Park in Didsbury, there was no running water or heating in the changing rooms, and the club didn't have the money to fix that, so the players often had to wash in the duck pond after games!

Nothing, however, was going to stop the Lancashire lasses from playing the game they loved. Not cold showers, not boggy pitches, not even the lack of local leagues. Because if Corinthians couldn't find enough opponents in their own county, then they would just have to travel elsewhere . . .

For the first few years, the team just toured around Britain – North, South, Midlands, Scotland – winning every cup or trophy on offer. *But what about the FA ban?* you might be wondering. Well, they were OK as long as their matches were raising money for charity. As the historian Jean Williams puts it, 'the Corinthians earned their right to play football by doing good.'

But don't be fooled by the poor facilities and 'friendly' games; Manchester Corinthians were a serious football club. Ashley and coach Derek Ingham weren't messing around on the muddy pitches at Fog Lane Park. They were running proper coaching sessions with skills, drills and tactical plans. Although most of the players had jobs and busy lives, they were still expected to turn up on time for training and matches every Sunday. And if they didn't, they would be dropped!

By 1957, the team was ready to travel overseas and take on more challenging opponents. The first Corinthians tour was to Portugal, organised by the International Red Cross charity, and the next was to Germany. There, they competed in an unofficial European Women's Championship against teams from Austria, Luxembourg, the Netherlands and West Germany, and guess who won? That's right . . .

Manchester Corinthians!

They even thrashed the German team 4–0 in the final, in front of 40,000 fans. Hurray, at last they felt like real football heroes!

After that, the Corinthians' international adventures continued: Portugal again in 1958, the Netherlands in 1959, and then in 1960, a three-month tour of South America and the Caribbean!

They were life-changing experiences for the Corinthians players, especially as so many of them were so young. One player, Margaret 'Titch' Wilde even joined the team aged twelve!

**'HAVING PREVIOUSLY PLAYED AT SPORTS GROUNDS IN ENGLAND, WHEN WE WENT ABROAD IT WAS COMPLETELY DIFFERENT AND FELT VERY PROFESSIONAL'**

– Margaret 'Whitty' Whitworth

By now, Corinthians were not just Britain's best women's football team; they were one of the best women's football teams in the world. The club proudly claimed to be 'Unbeaten by any foreign team at home or abroad', with a run of 141 games without defeat. Beat that, Dick, Kerr Ladies!

But just as Corinthians reached the peak of their powers, the women's game began to change. When England won the FIFA World Cup in 1966, it was a moment that inspired not just male footballers, but female footballers too. Suddenly, more and more women and girls were getting into the game . . . and wondering why they weren't allowed to play on proper pitches like the men and boys.

In 1969, the Women's Football Association was formed, and two years later in 1971, the Men's FA finally agreed to lift the ban. At last, after fifty years of unfair treatment, female footballers were free to play wherever they wanted!

It was great news for the women's game, but not such

great news for Manchester Corinthians. After one last big European tournament win in 1970, their successful run came to an end. When the first Women's FA Cup final took place the following year, Corinthians could no longer call themselves the best team in Britain; that was winners Southampton, followed by the Scottish runners-up Stewarton Thistle. In fact, Corinthians weren't even the best team in the North West any more; that was Fodens Ladies!

It was a sad and swift decline for such a famous team, but Corinthians would always be remembered for playing a crucial role in keeping the women's game going during the dark days of the FA ban. What an exciting time they'd had together, touring the world, and what excellent players they'd helped to produce.

In November 1972, England took on Scotland in their first-ever international match. From 2–0 down, the Lionesses fought back to win 3–2, inspired by a bursting solo run from midfielder Sylvia Gore, who dribbled all the way from her own half to score her country's first-

ever international goal. And where had Gore spent the first six years of her football career? Yes, at Manchester Corinthians, of course!

**'WE PLAYED ALL OVER THE WORLD. AS A YOUNGSTER I PLAYED IN FRONT OF 80,000 IN SOUTH AMERICA AND AT THE SAN SIRO STADIUM IN MILAN'**

– Sylvia Gore

The Rise and Fall – and Rise Again – of Brazil's Brilliant Black Footballers

No other country plays football, and loves football, quite like Brazil. The South Americans have won the World Cup five times, more than any other nation, and they have produced superstar after superstar, from Pelé, 'the King of Football', through to Neymar and Vinícius Júnior, passing through Ronaldo, Ronaldinho and Marta along the way.

As well as their fantastic samba skills, these football heroes also have something else in common: they all come from backgrounds that are not white. Brazil has a large population of Black people for several reasons, one of which is sugar and slavery. By the 1500s, sugar had become popular in Europe, and in order to make enough of it, white traders transported more than five million enslaved Africans to Brazil in ships to work in

terrible conditions on the sugar-cane plantations.

Shockingly, slavery didn't stop in Brazil until 1888, and when it did, the Black population still continued to suffer horrible discrimination. They were only allowed to do the lowest jobs, they couldn't vote, they couldn't own a house, and at first, they couldn't even play football . . .

When the beautiful game first arrived in Brazil in the 1890s, it came from Britain and was seen as another sport for wealthy white people to enjoy, just like rugby and cricket. These rich men formed fancy clubs to keep others out – but as we've said before, the great thing about football is you don't need a perfect grass pitch to play on, and you don't need lots of expensive equipment. So, by the 1910s, the game had spread far and wide, becoming Brazil's most popular sport, among both the rich and the poor. A game for everyone.

However, despite their growing flair and passion for football, Brazilian players were only welcome at the big clubs or in the national team if they were white. When Arthur Friedenreich, the son of a white German father and a Black Brazilian mother, played for Brazil at the 1919 South American Championships, he had to try and hide his heritage from the fans by flattening his hair before games. Sadly, once he got out on to the pitch, Friedenreich was fouled again and again, and the referee did nothing about it. Some say that's where Brazil's skilful style of football, the *jogo bonito* ('beautiful game'), began. Because Friedenreich had to dip and swerve as he dribbled with the ball, to dodge the dirty tackles.

In the 1930s, the situation improved a little for Brazil's Black footballers, with a few shining brightly on the game's greatest stage. Fausto was a key member of the 1930 World Cup team. In 1938, Domingos da Guia was their star defender and Leônidas da Silva became the tournament's best player and top scorer. In Brazil's opening game against Poland, Leônidas scored a stunning hat-trick, including the winning goal. The best bit? He

scored wearing only his socks after getting his boot stuck in the mud! According to one journalist, 'Each time he touched the ball there was an electric current of enthusiasm through the crowd.'

Match by match, the Brazilian people grew prouder and prouder of their national team, and they began to wonder if the diversity of their team was something they should celebrate, rather than hide.

Unfortunately, the lovely idea of a united Brazil didn't last very long. In the 1950 World Cup final, the national team suffered a shocking home defeat to their rivals Uruguay. The match was known as *'El Maracanaço'*, after the Maracanã Stadium where it took place.

With ten minutes to go, Brazil were on their way to their first World Cup trophy, when suddenly disaster struck.

I'll let football writer Alex Bellos describe the moment for you: '[Alcides] Ghiggia again dribbled past Bigode and entered the box. Instead of crossing . . . Ghiggia shot immediately to the near post. The angle was tight.

Barbosa was caught off guard. He dived to his left but was too late.'

Brazil had lost the 1950 World Cup final! *Nooo!*

And who got the worst of the blame? Their midfielder Bigode, their left-back Juvenal, and their goalkeeper Barbosa. OK, so all three players could perhaps have done a bit better to stop the goal, but they also had something else in common: they were all Black Brazilians. Suddenly, the country weren't feeling so proud of their racial mix anymore. Although Barbosa was named the best goalkeeper at the World Cup, he only played one more game for the national team.

Four years later, Brazil suffered another shocking defeat, this time in the quarter-finals against Hungary. By the time the 1958 World Cup came round, their manager Vicente Feola decided to pick players known for their calm and experience, and so he left the team's two most exciting stars on the bench: a tricky winger called Garrincha and a 17-year-old striker who you might have heard of, called Pelé!

> **'YOUNG, TALENTED, INVENTIVE; GARRINCHA AND PELÉ REFLECTED A BRAZIL WITH A PROMISING FUTURE. FOR THE MANAGERS, HOWEVER, THEY REMAINED "NON-WHITE" PLAYERS FIRST'**
>
> – Mickaël Correia

Yes, Brazil's Black footballers were being discriminated against, again. According to tests done by João Carvalhaes, the new team psychologist, Garrincha, who came from an American Indian family, lacked aggression and intelligence, while Pelé, who was Afro-Brazilian, lacked 'the necessary fighting spirit and doesn't have the sense of responsibility that is essential for any team game'. Really, you sure about that, João? He would be turn out to be very wrong . . .

After a 3–0 win over Austria and then a boring 0–0 draw with England, the fans and players called for change. 'We want Garrincha and Pelé to play!' And when they did, Brazil became UNSTOPPABLE. *Jogo bonito* was really born.

Against the Soviet Union, Garrincha hit the left post in the first minute, then Pelé hit the right post in the second, before their teammate Vavá finally scored in the third. According to Bellos, 'They are considered by many as Brazilian football's **greatest three minutes of all time**.'

But the beautiful, winning football didn't stop there:

*Quarter-finals – Brazil 1 Wales 0* – winner scored by . . . Pelé!

*Semi-finals – Brazil 5 France 2* – hat-trick for Pelé!

*Final – Brazil 5 Sweden 2* – another amazing hat-trick for Pelé, plus two terrific assists for Garrincha!

At last, they had done it; Brazil had won the World Cup! And with their sublime skills, Pelé and Garrincha had proved the racists wrong.

Four years later, Brazil won it again. This time, Garrincha stepped up to be the team's leading superstar, after Pelé suffered an early injury. By 1970, Garrincha was no longer part of the national team, but don't worry,

Pelé was still there to complete a different kind of hat-trick: three World Cup trophies!

## 'WITH PELÉ AND GARRINCHA PLAYING TOGETHER, THE NATIONAL TEAM NEVER LOST A MATCH'

**– Alex Bellos**

Those World Cup wins helped create a new national pride, and a new national identity that celebrated the country's unique diversity. Football was a game for everyone, and Brazil was a nation for everyone. The victories also helped inspire future generations of brilliant Black Brazilian footballers, who have kept the success going: Romário and Cafu in 1994, and then the 'Three Rs', Ronaldo, Ronaldinho and Rivaldo in 2002.

So, who will be next? Will it be Vinícius Júnior and Endrick in 2026? Or maybe Kerolin and Geyse at the Women's World Cup in 2027? Whoever it is, you can be sure they'll play the beautiful game the beautiful Brazilian way.

## Get Ready for . . . the RoboCup!

A game for everyone, eh?

Even animals? Yes, in 2021, a dog ran on to the pitch during a league match in Chile, South America, and scored!

Even robots? Yes, football has got them covered too, with their very own special tournament. Say hello to . . . the RoboCup!

It all started in the mid-1990s, with the 'Robot World Cup Initiative', a project created by a group of university professors, with the aim that: 'By the middle of the 21st century, a team of fully autonomous humanoid robot soccer players shall win a soccer game, complying with the rules of FIFA, against the winner of the most recent World Cup.'

Really?! I'd love to see a team of machines try to stop Lionel Messi's Argentina, wouldn't you?

In 1997, IBM's super-computer 'Deep Blue' managed to defeat Garry Kasparov, the human world champion in chess, so why couldn't they do the same with football?

To reach their ambitious goal, however, the professors were going to need plenty of help. So, they decided to set up a yearly event where the best robot teams from all over the world could compete against each other and share their amazing ideas. A World Cup but for robot footballers – what should they call it?

The first-ever RoboCup took place in Japan in 1997, with thirty-eight robot teams from eleven different countries, and five thousand fans cheering them on at the Nagoya Congress Center. By Singapore 2010, the tournament had grown to five hundred teams from forty countries! Now, there are national cups in Portugal, Brazil, China and Germany, as well as lots of local leagues.

Oh and listen up, because there's also a RoboCupJunior! But back to the main event: a few months after the 2022 FIFA World Cup in Qatar, the 2022 RoboCup was held in Bangkok, Thailand, and the winners were 'B-Human', created by a team of students from the University of Bremen in Germany and the German Research Center for Artificial Intelligence. On their way to the trophy, 'B-Human' even achieved two things that Messi's Argentina failed to do:

    1) They won every single game
    2) They didn't concede a single goal

Hmmm, maybe it might be a decent match, after all.

And thanks to competitions such as RoboCup, the bots are getting bigger and better. Researchers at the University of California, Los Angeles recently created a new 1.4 m humanoid (something that looks like a human, but isn't) called Artemis that can run, as well as walk and jump.

Why 'Artemis'? Well, it's short for:

A
Robot
That
Exceeds
Messi
In
Soccer

Really, a robot that's better than Messi?! We'll see about that . . .

# FULL TIME!

*Take a deep breath, stretch those legs and then join the team huddle, because we're heading into . . .*

EXTRA TIME!

# CHAPTER SEVEN

## CHANGING THINGS FOR THE BETTER

Now, seeing as football is a game for everyone and enjoyed by so many, it also has the power to **impact the lives of billions of people**. In difficult times, it can help bring **joy and hope**, and in frustrating times, it can provide the push that turns the wheels of progress. Yes, football and footballers really can **change the world**, and here are three more unbelievable stories to prove it.

People often talk about football as 'the global game', but what does that *really* mean? Well, if you want a perfect example, then look no further than the extraordinary life story of Awer Mabil.

It starts on 15 September 1995, the day he was born in a refugee camp in the African country of Kenya. A violent civil war had forced Awer's parents to flee their homeland of Sudan, and travel south in search of food and shelter for their family. Eventually, they found a small hut to call their home at the Kakuma refugee camp, and that's where they lived for the first ten years of Awer's life.

It was a difficult start, full of setbacks and struggle. But Mabil learned a lot of important lessons during that time: about staying positive, about staying humble, and about playing football.

Awer's first experiences of the game came on the dirt pitches at Kakuma, where the barefoot kids spent their days kicking footballs that they made out of rolled-up socks, plastic bags and balloons. The more Mabil played, the more he loved it . . . and the more he practised, the better he became! With his speed and skill, he was unstoppable on the attack!

In 2006, Awer and his family finally got the good news they'd been waiting years for: they would be leaving the camp in Kenya and moving to . . . Adelaide, in South Australia!

Gulp! A new home in a new country on a new continent, with a new language and a completely different way of life – it was a lot of big changes to get used to, especially when you're only ten years old. But Awer wasn't going to let anything stop him. Plus, there was one comforting thing that linked his old life in Kakuma with his new one in Adelaide: football.

**'Football,' Mabil says, 'is the world game, a language everybody speaks.'**

Through the beautiful game, he was able to communicate with his new neighbours and classmates, and that really helped him settle in. At his new school, he was also introduced to lots of other sports such as cricket, Aussie rules and rugby union. But football was still his favourite. That was the game he wanted to play for the rest of his life, and at the highest level possible: yes, the FIFA World Cup!

From his new home in Adelaide, Awer was able to watch the 2006 tournament on TV – Australia's amazing comeback against Japan, the many high-pressure penalty shoot-outs, and of course, Zinedine Zidane's famous head-butt in the final . . .

Wow, what entertainment! The whole event turned out to be an incredibly inspiring experience for him.

**'He had a dream that one day . . . he would play at a World Cup and he would represent Australia,'** said Mabil's uncle Peter Kuereng.

At first, Awer made his way up through the local

leagues, until in 2012, his special talent was spotted by Adelaide United, a professional club in the A-League, Australia's top division. A year later, aged 17, he made his senior debut on the right wing, and soon scored his first goal.

Woah, what next for Australia's new soccer superstar?

Well, in 2015, Awer decided to follow in the footsteps of countrymen like Tim Cahill, Mark Schwarzer and Aaron Mooy, by setting off for Europe. He started the next part of his football journey in Denmark, with FC Midtjylland, where he scored in the UEFA Champions League against Ajax. Hurray! He then moved on to more adventures in Portugal, Turkey, Spain, the Czech Republic and Switzerland.

But what about Awer's Australia dream?

Well, Mabil made his senior international debut in 2018, a few months after the World Cup in Russia, and then starred for 'the Socceroos' (the nickname of the Australian national team) at the 2019 AFC Asian Cup. Next, could he make his other football dream come true by helping his country qualify for the 2022 World Cup in Qatar?

With goals against China and Oman, Awer got Australia off to a great start, but ultimately, they finished third in Group B, behind Japan and Saudi Arabia. Oh well, they would just have to get to the World Cup the hard way! Through two extra must-win matches:

## 1) The Asian Football Confederation (AFC) decider

Thanks to a late goal from Ajdin Hrustić, Australia won 2–1 against the United Arab Emirates to reach . . .

## 2) The World Cup qualification play-off

There, Australia faced Peru, the fifth-best team from South America. When Awer came on as a sub in the 70th minute, the score was still 0–0 – so, could he make the difference for his country? Not at first, no. Bursting forward with speed, Mabil set up left-back Aziz Behich, who curled a shot wide, and then Hrustić, who hit the ball straight at the keeper.

*90 minutes played, still 0–0.*

*120 minutes played, still 0–0.*

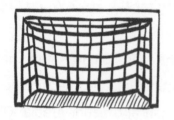

*You know what that means . . .* **PENALTIES!**

Awer wasn't selected as one of Australia's first five takers, but he still had a key part to play. Because after one miss each, the shoot-out went all the way to . . . SUDDEN DEATH!

Sounds super-scary, doesn't it? And it is – basically, if you miss and the other team scores, it's all over and you lose. So as Awer stepped up for Australia, the pressure was really on. But he kept calm and held his nerve. With a skip and then two quick steps, he . . . placed his shot in the bottom corner, sending the keeper the wrong way. *GOAL!*

As he turned away, Awer punched the air with pride, and moments later, he was celebrating even more because the Australia keeper Andrew Redmayne saved the next Peru penalty. Hurray, it was all over and the Socceroos were on their way to the 2022 World Cup!

While his teammates jumped up and down together,

Awer knelt on the grass next to them, crying tears of pure joy.

'I knew I was going to score,' Mabil said after the match. 'It was the only way to say thank you to Australia on behalf of my family.'

And that's not the only way he has given back to the places that helped shape him. In 2014, Mabil returned to Kenya with his elder brother, Awer Bul, to give twenty football shirts and some leather footballs to young refugees at the camp where they'd lived. But that was just the beginning. They were determined to do more to change the world for the better, so, a year later, they set up the charity 'Barefoot to Boots'.

This organisation empowers refugees by giving them the things they need to play the game they love, including football boots, shirts and balls (there is now a Kakuma Premier League for men's and women's teams). They also provide health and education resources to build a brighter future for the refugees and their families.

'When they see a young man achieve what Awer has

done it brings their dreams to reality,' says Ian Smith, the chairman of the charity. 'It's a way out, it's a way forward.'

Speaking of bringing dreams to reality, we'll end this story on 22 November 2023, when, in the 73rd minute of Australia's match against France, Mabil ran on to the field to add a new line to his amazing list of achievements:

> *Professional footballer*
>
> *Australia international*
>
> *Australia Cup winner*
>
> *Danish league winner*
>
> *Czech league winner*
>
> *Champions League goalscorer*
>
> *La Liga player*
>
> and now, at last . . .

*World Cup player!* From Kenya to Qatar: Awer's incredible football journey was complete.

# Las 15 Who Fought for a Better Football World and Won

While the women's game has made massive progress over the last twenty years, the fight for equality still goes on. Female footballers still earn a lot less money, receive a lot less support, and suffer more discrimination. But why should they be treated any differently to their male colleagues, when they do the same job?

Luckily, things are starting to change for the better thanks to the actions of inspirational players. Just like the fifteen brave Spanish players who agreed to stand up, speak out and stop playing for their national team in protest at the inequality they faced.

*Las 15* sent their joint letter to the Royal Spanish Football Federation (RFEF) in September 2022, but really, the problems they wrote about had been going on for years. While the Spain men's team were winning

Euro 2008 and the 2010 World Cup, their women's team were failing to even qualify for Euro 2009 and the 2011 World Cup. At last, in 2013, La Roja ('The Reds') had reached a major international tournament, but their record remained disappointing:

*Euro 2013 – knocked out in the quarter-finals*
*2015 World Cup – knocked out in the group stage*
*Euro 2017 – knocked out in the quarter-finals*
*2019 World Cup – knocked out in the Round of 16 . . .*

But why? Was it a question of talent?

No way! By the time Euro 2022 kicked off, Spain had one of the best squads in women's football. Nine of their players had been part of the brilliant Barcelona team that won the UEFA Women's Champions League in 2021, while their star midfielder, Alexia Putellas, had just won the Women's Ballon d'Or.

And yet, at the tournament in England, La Roja struggled to find any rhythm. Were these the same skilful players that shone so brightly for their clubs? Spain only got through the group stage thanks to a last-minute winner against Denmark, and then they lost in the quarter-finals . . . AGAIN.

So, if bad players weren't the problem, then what was wrong?

Short answer: everything else! Many felt that under manager Jorge Vilda, the team's preparation had been poor and unprofessional, and the atmosphere in the camp had been far from positive. The players felt they needed a fresh start, and so in August 2022, the three captains Irene Paredes, Jenni Hermoso and Patricia Guijarro went to speak to Vilda and told him that the team 'believed a change was needed in both training and tactics'.

They also spoke to RFEF President Luis Rubiales, but things stayed exactly the same: same unhappy environment, same unpopular manager.

With the 2023 Women's World Cup coming up, what were the players going to do now? Well, on 23 September 2022, the RFEF received fifteen emails from fifteen of their top female footballers:

Barcelona stars **Aitana Bonmatí**, **Mariona Caldentey**, **Patricia Guijarro**, **Mapi León**, **Sandra Paños** and **Clàudia Pina**; Atlético Madrid stars **Lola Gallardo** and **Ainhoa Moraza**; Real Sociedad stars **Nerea Eizagirre** and **Amaiur Sarriegi**; **Ona Batlle** and **Lucía García** of Manchester United; **Laia Aleixandri** and **Leila Ouahabi** of Manchester City; and **Andrea Perreira** from Mexico team Club América.

Each email contained exactly the same message: they wanted the team culture to *change*, and until it did, they would stop playing for Spain.

With Putellas and Irene Paredes also adding their support via social media, the players were applying serious pressure. But would it result in any positive change? Not at first . . . The RFEF refused to listen to their requests, and in their next matches against Sweden and the USA, Spain simply played on without them.

So, who would give in first: the RFEF or *Las 15*? When

it became clear that the players were sticking together, the federation agreed to make some changes ahead of the 2023 Women's World Cup in Australia and New Zealand:

1. More flights, rather than long, uncomfortable coach journeys
2. More technical staff to support the team, rather than players looking after themselves

It was progress, but was it *enough* progress to persuade the players to come back?

In March 2023, Putellas and Paredes both returned to the Spain squad, along with three from *Las 15*: Bonmatí, Caldentey and Batlle. The other twelve, however, continued to say no, even as the World Cup grew closer and closer. Would Spain have to try and win the tournament without them?

Yes, and they still succeeded. The twenty-three players in the Spain squad put their protests to one side and showed real strength and team spirit. After a shock 4–0 defeat to Japan in the group stage, La Roja bounced back to reach their full potential on the pitch at last.

They thrashed Switzerland 5–1 in the Round of 16 . . . edged past the Netherlands in extra-time in the quarters . . . scored a last-minute winner against Sweden in the semis . . . and then held their nerve to beat England 1–0 in the final.

Hurray, despite everything that had happened, Spain had done it . . . They were the new champions of the world!

And what an incredible team effort it had been. From rising star Salma Paralluelo to captain and scorer of the World Cup-winning goal, Olga Carmona, and not forgetting Bonmatí, an original member of *Las 15* who was awarded the Golden Ball for the tournament's Best Player. Together, they had all made their international football dream come true.

I'd love to end this story on that positive note, but sadly, that success led to more problems for Spain to solve. Because as the players walked up to collect their winners' medals, Rubiales was there on the stage to congratulate them, and when it was Hermoso's turn, he hugged her tightly and then suddenly kissed her on the lips.

Woah, was that really appropriate behaviour from the RFEF President?! Would Rubiales have treated one of Spain's male football stars in that way? Most people agreed that the answer to both questions was a big, loud **'NO'**. Critics described it as blatant discrimination, and it left Hermoso feeling disrespected, as both a player and a person.

'I didn't expect it,' she said months later. 'I didn't do anything to land myself in that situation . . . how could I expect it in that scenario of a medal ceremony at a World Cup final?'

After taking a few small steps forward, the RFEF had just taken one giant leap backwards. It was clear that Spanish football still needed to make much bigger changes for the better. Five days later, Rubiales resigned, and two weeks later, Vilda was sacked too.

At last, it was time for the fresh start that *Las 15* had been calling for.

Pedro Rocha took over as RFEF President and made a public apology. Montserrat Tomé, meanwhile, became the new national team manager, and their first-ever female coach.

Again, it was progress, but was it enough progress to please the players? No, *Las 15*, together with most of Spain's World Cup-winning squad, wanted more, much more. 'We firmly believe that strong changes are required in leadership positions in the RFEF and specifically, in the area of women's football,' they said in a powerful joint statement.

Wow, thirty-nine footballers all refusing to play for their country – uh-oh, if they didn't act fast, Spain were going to have to field a C Team for their next game against Sweden! The RFEF quickly arranged a meeting with the players, and they agreed to make major changes straight away.

Deal! Spain's top female footballers accepted the

offer and twenty-one of them returned in time to play against Sweden. Before the match, the two teams stood together as one, holding a banner that read,

> **'#SeAcabó ('It's Over')**
> **Our fight is the global fight'**

Thanks to the brave, bold action of *Las 15* and the twenty-four others that joined them later, the Spanish women's national team had finally won their battle to – in the words of Paredes – 'play football in appropriate conditions where we are respected.' Doesn't sound like too much to ask, does it? And yet it feels like real progress at last.

Out on the football pitch, no player runs more than a central midfielder. James Ward-Prowse, Declan Rice, Bruno Guimaraes – these guys run from box to box, all game long, with hardly any rest in between. So, how do they do it? Well, for most midfielders the answer is lots of fitness

work in the gym, but for **Marshall Munetsi**, the answer is a little more complicated, and a lot more interesting.

Munetsi now plays in France, for Ligue 1 club Stade de Reims (you may have heard of their manager, Will Still, who first developed his coaching skills by playing the *Football Manager* video games!), but he comes from Zimbabwe, a country in Southern Africa.

When it first became an independent nation in 1980, Zimbabwe was described as 'the Jewel of Africa'. But by the time Munetsi was born in 1996, the future didn't look so bright at all. Under President Robert Mugabe, thousands of people in the south-west region of Matabeleland had been killed for protesting against the government, there were huge health problems across the country, and the people were getting poorer.

Growing up in Harare, Zimbabwe's capital city, Munetsi and his family experienced very tough times, but he was determined to one day fulfil his dream of becoming a professional footballer.

'Really, a footballer?' his mother wondered and worried.

'But why – is it just because of the money and fame?'

No, it wasn't that at all! Marshall loved playing the game, and he also wanted to use the power of sport to help people in need.

'Being a voice for others is something that's been with me since school when I was deputy head boy,' he says. So, he promised his mother that, 'any platform I developed would be used to make a positive change in this world.'

Deal! With his family's support, Munetsi set off for South Africa to kickstart his professional football career. In 2015, he signed for second division club Ubuntu Cape Town, and two years later, he was playing for Orlando Pirates, one of the top teams in the whole of Africa.

Next step? Europe!

Yes, in 2019, Reims came calling and Marshall got his dream-move to France. He would now be playing against world-class players like Neymar Jr, Cesc Fàbregas and Dimitri Payet every week! So, would he fall for the money and fame as so many other footballers had, or would he

continue to make his mother proud?

On the pitch, Munetsi worked harder than ever in midfield to win the ball back for his new team, putting in a man-of-the-match performance in a 2–0 win against Neymar Jr's PSG.

And off the pitch, he worked harder than ever to give back to his community, by starting his own charity, the 'Marshall Munetsi Foundation'. Yes, he was now a football star in France, but Marshall hadn't forgotten the struggling country that he came from, or his promise to his mother. So, he decided that he would donate 10 per cent of his Reims wages to his foundation, 'to provide underprivileged children in Zimbabwe with the tools and resources they need to succeed. Through education, mentorship, and opportunity.'

**'WE DESERVE THE MONEY WE EARN, BUT WHAT DO WE DO WITH IT? I WANT TO CHANGE THE WORLD.'**

– Marshall Munetsi

At the end of his first season, Reims gave Munetsi a new four-year contract, calling him an 'impact player and delightful man'. It meant more money and more fame, but he just carried on his hard and humble work, both on and off the pitch.

Tackles, blocks, interceptions, ball recoveries – Marshall did it all in defensive midfield, and he still had the energy to race forward and join the Reims attack too. He scored his first Ligue 1 goal during the 2020–21 season . . .

. . . then five in 2021–22 . . .

. . . then seven in 2022–23, to go with four assists!

After such an excellent season, Marshall was attracting plenty of attention from English Premier League clubs, but Reims came up with a clever plan to keep hold of their key midfielder. They rewarded Munetsi by offering him a new contract, which included a very special new bonus scheme: for every kilometre he ran during matches, the club would donate €100 to his foundation.

Wow, for a hard-working midfielder like Marshall, that was going to add up to a lot of money – more than €1,000 per game! In one record-setting match against Rennes, he had even run 13.72 km in 90 minutes.

'When I heard about the clause, I didn't need to ask any more questions,' he said. 'I told my agent immediately that I wanted to sign because this was the kind of club that I wanted to play for; one that looks to improve the lives of others and one that helps me to be both a player and person that my mother can be proud of.'

Deal done! Reims announced the great news with a video and the message, 'To find a better source of motivation, you can always run.'

So, with the extra motivation, how far would Munetsi go? For the next match against Lille, the club put a kilometre counter on the big screen in the stadium, so all the supporters could see how far he had run.

'Keep going, Marshall!' the fans cried, cheering him on to run even further.

At the final whistle, it was Reims 1 Lille 0, and who scored the winner? Yep, you guessed it: Munetsi, with a heroic diving header!

And just as importantly, he had also run over 13 km – for his team and for his charity! Yes, for you clever clogs, that makes €13,000 for that game alone!

With the extra money raised, the Marshall Munetsi Foundation is now able to pay the school fees for sixty local kids, rather than thirty, and the more the midfielder runs, the higher that number will rise. So, keep going, Marshall – we're with you every step of the way!

# The Last Country in the World Without a National Football Team

For this next story, we're moving from one amazing Marshall to another: the Marshall Islands.

Have you heard of them? Don't worry if you haven't. It's not like they've ever competed at a FIFA World Cup before, or at any other major international tournament. In fact, in 2020, the Marshall Islands called themselves the last country in the world without a national football team!

There are a few good reasons for it:

1) Only just over forty-two thousand people live there, putting it at number twenty in the list of the world's smallest countries by population. Plus, those forty-two thousand people are spread across five different islands, so it's not the easiest place to form a football team.

2) The Marshall Islands lie way out in the middle of the Northwestern Pacific Ocean, with the Philippines to the west, Hawaii to the east, the South Pacific islands of Fiji and Vanuatu to the south. And to the north? Just miles and miles of empty sea! So, it's not that straightforward for other football teams to get to either.

3) The Marshall Islands have close ties with the USA, which means their most popular sports are baseball and basketball. Oh, and because they're surrounded by water, they also love swimming! So, it's not exactly the easiest place to find enough people who really want to play football.

In 2020, however, the Marshall Islands Soccer Federation (MISF) set out to change all that. But, what would they need to start a national football team?

- **A coach** – *tick!* They hired an Englishman called Lloyd Owers to be their Technical Director
- **A stadium** – *tick!* It was agreed that they could play matches at the national stadium, the Majuro Track and Field Stadium
- **A kit** – *tick!* In March 2023, the federation ran a competition to design the team's first kit. The winner was Micael Altarimano from Argentina, who created a shirt of true football beauty: ocean blue with spiky orange and white stripes, to match the colours of the national flag. The kit is also made from recycled plastic to raise awareness of climate change, which is a massive problem for the Marshall Islands

Right, on to the more difficult stuff:

- **A team of talented players** – hmmm, let's just call that a work in progress

Owers began training up the best local footballers, and meanwhile he hired an American man called Pat McStay to scout for any players in the USA who might have Marshallese parents or grandparents.

- **Opponents to play against** – arghhh, this turned out to be the hardest part of all!

The Marshall Islands aim to join the Oceania Football Confederation (OFC) and compete against countries such as New Zealand and Fiji, before then becoming a FIFA member and trying to qualify for the World Cup. That will take time and a lot of small steps, though, starting with a first-ever international match.

At one point, it looked like they might play at the 2023 Micronesian Games, but in the end, the tournament was cancelled. Because the team wasn't ready yet? No, because all the hotels on the islands were already fully booked!

The MISF President Shev Livai has now put forward a more realistic goal: the 2027 Pacific Games. That gives more time for the team to build a strong squad of players, and more time for us football fans to buy the beautiful shirts, supporting the world's newest national team. Come on, you Marshall Islands!

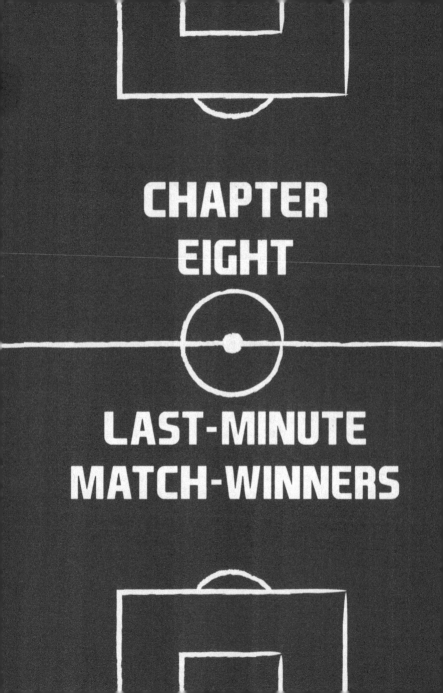

# CHAPTER EIGHT

# LAST-MINUTE MATCH-WINNERS

Can you believe it, we're almost out of time and space . . . again! But don't go shaking hands, swapping shirts, and moving on to the next book just yet. Remember, it's not over until the final whistle blows/page turns.

On the touchline, the fourth official is holding up the electronic board to indicate . . .

**THREE MORE STORIES IN ADDED TIME!**

(Plus a *Weird & Wonderful*, of course.)

Hurray, and have we got a nail-biting final section for you! We're talking super-exciting moments at the very end of massive football matches, involving:

- Big decisions and even bigger drama
- Iconic scenes of joy and despair
- Two ice-cold penalty kicks that changed football forever

But first, two late, *LAAAATE* Manchester City goals that won more than just a football match . . .

If you're fairly new to football or new to being a Manchester City fan, you may not realise just how average the club used to be. Yes, there were some golden spells, but from the late 1970s to 2008, there was a long period of pain, frustration and frequent relegation.

So, what happened in 2009 to turn things around? Well, that's when Manchester City Football Club was bought by the Abu Dhabi United Group owned by Sheikh Mansour bin Zayed Al Nahyan, the vice president of a country called the United Arab Emirates, and a member of the Abu Dhabi royal family.

When Sheikh Mansour first took over, however, City fans knew very little about him. In fact, they only really knew two things for sure:

1) He had LOTS of money

2) He was VERY willing to spend it

His shopping list looked a bit like this:

- £32.5 million on Brazilian winger Robinho
- £18 million on Brazilian striker Jô
- £16 million on Dutch midfielder Nigel de Jong
- £14 million on Welsh striker Craig Bellamy. . .

And that wasn't even half of City's signings during that wild, first season!

All that buying didn't bring instant success, though. The club finished tenth in the Premier League in 2009, then fifth in 2010. By 2011, however, City were finally ready to compete for major trophies, and take on their local rivals, United.

Since the early 1990s, United had been by far the best team in Manchester, and the best team in the whole of England too. In twenty years, they had won twelve Premier League titles, as well as four FA Cups, four League Cups, and two Champions League trophies.

And City? They had won one league title . . . in the Second Division (now called the Championship)!

All that was about to change, though. Under new manager, Roberto Mancini, City were starting to look like the real deal, with Vincent Kompany in defence, Yaya Touré and David Silva in midfield, and a superstar strikeforce featuring:

- Argentinians Sergio Agüero and Carlos Tevez
- The big Bosnian Edin Džeko
- The unpredictable Italian Mario Balotelli (if you read *Unbelievable Football 2*, you'll know he volunteered at a dog rescue centre, and also burned down his bathroom after setting off fireworks inside his own house!)

In their first year together, City's new team won the FA Cup, beating Stoke City 1–0 in the final. But now they wanted more . . . During the 2011–12 season, they wanted to challenge United for the Premier League title.

After ten games, City were top of the table, five points ahead of United. After twenty games, they were still top, but only by three points now. After thirty games, they had slipped down to second.

Oh dear, title race over? Not yet. In the final weeks of the season, United stumbled, and when City kept on winning, they took over the top spot again. Now, with one game to go, all they had to do was beat relegation strugglers QPR at home, and they would be Champions of England for the first time since 1968!

Doesn't sound too difficult, right? Wrong!

At half-time, City were 1–0 up with the title in sight, but as the pressure built up, so did the mistakes in their defence . . .

Joleon Lescott got his header all wrong, allowing Djibril Cissé to race through and equalise. *1–1!*

Then, with QPR down to ten men after another moment of madness from Joey Barton, City failed to take advantage. Instead, they let Jamie Mackie sneak in unmarked at the back post to score with a diving header. *2–1 to QPR!*

Noooooooooo, what on earth was going on? On the last day, they were throwing the title away! United were winning 1–0 away at Sunderland, which meant they

would be crowned Premier League champions again . . . unless City could somehow score two more goals.

Two more goals – OK, so where were they going to come from?

Agüero, City's top scorer, was having a fairly quiet game, but Mancini knew all he needed was half a chance, so he left him on the pitch.

Hmmm, who else could he call on? In the 69th minute, the City manager sent on Džeko to replace defensive midfielder Gareth Barry. And in the 75th minute, he brought on Balotelli for Tevez.

So, would they turn out to be super-subs or blooper-subs? At first, things didn't look good. Džeko hit the post from close range, and then Balotelli headed the ball straight at the QPR keeper.

Arghhh, how many more chances would City get to save the title?! Soon, the 90 minutes were up; now all they had left was FIVE minutes of injury time . . .

'I thought it was all over,' Agüero admitted later. 'How could we find two goals in the time that remained?'

*Come on, City!*

### Minute One

Silva dribbles forward on the right and slips a pass through for right-back Pablo Zabaleta on the run. His cross is blocked – *Corner!*

### Minute Two

Silva curls an absolute beauty into the crowded six-yard box, and up leaps Džeko, high above everyone else, to head the ball down into the net. *GOOOOOOAL – 2–2!*

Hurray, he's a super-sub, after all! There's no time for celebrations, though, because City still need another to win the league . . .

### Minute Three

Instead of trying to keep the ball like any smart team would do with seconds left, QPR decide to just launch it forward and give it straight back to City. Thanks! Lescott heads it to de Jong, who plays the ball through to Agüero, who has dropped deep to receive it . . .

### Minute Four

In a flash, Agüero turns and pokes a pass through

to Balotelli, who uses his strength to hold the ball up and then slide it back to Agüero for the one-two. The Argentinian is into the box now, where he skips past one last lunging tackle, and then steadies himself to take the most important shot of his football career so far.

**'THIS WAS IT, THE ONE CHANCE I'D HOPED WOULD COME AND I HAD TO MAKE IT COUNT, SO I HIT THE BALL AS HARD AS I COULD AND HOPED FOR THE BEST'**

**– Sergio Agüero**

*BANG! . . . GOOOOOOOOOOAAAAAAAAAL – 3–2!*

**'I don't remember anything immediately after, but when it sank in, I realised I'd scored the best goal of my life.'**

No problem, let me fill you in, Sergio. As the City fans and players go wild all around him, Agüero whips his shirt off and swings it above his head like a lasso.

If you haven't heard the classic TV commentary, it goes a little something like this:

'Balotelli . . . AgueeeeeerooooooooOOOOOOOOOOOOOOOOOOO! I swear you'll never see anything like this ever again. So watch it, drink it in.'

Last-minute match-winners really don't get any better than that!

**Minute Five**

City take their sweet time at the back until . . .

### *FWEEEET!! – FINAL WHISTLE!*

Manchester City are the new Premier League Champions!

What follows are ABSOLUTE SCENES! As the City players celebrate together, thousands of supporters storm the pitch to join in too. It's all very lovely, if a little dangerous . . .

*Džeko – 92 mins*

*Agüero – 94 mins*

Those two injury-time goals changed everything for Manchester City. Not only did they win the club their first-ever Premier League title, but they also launched an exciting new era, leading to LOTS more trophies:

- Premier League titles in 2014, 2018, 2019, 2021 and 2022
- FA Cups in 2011 and 2019
- League Cups in 2014, 2016, 2018, 2019, 2020 and 2021

and then . . .

- 2023. The Treble: the Premier League, the FA Cup, and at last, the UEFA Champions League!

But if it wasn't for those dramatic late goals from Džeko and Agüero eleven years earlier, would City be where they are now? Would they have been able to sign world-class superstars like Kevin De Bruyne, Erling Haaland, Jack Grealish and Rodri? Good question, eh! You can probably guess what Agüero's answer would be, but who am I to argue with a City legend?

**'That season gave us more confidence because we had the players to win the title every year. That season was the start of it.'**

## A Cheeky Chip that Changed Penalties Forever

But what if there's no injury-time winner, and no goals in extra-time either? Well, then there's only one way to end the match, and this book: with . . . PENALTIES!

Picture this: you're about to step up and take a crucial spot-kick at the end of a long, tense shoot-out. There's a major trophy on the line, and you could be your team's hero! The atmosphere in the stadium is electric as you make the long walk forward and place the ball down on the spot. You know what you need to do – keep calm and score – but HOW are you going to do it?

*Power or placement? Top corner or bottom corner? Right or left?*

*Or, maybe, if you're feeling confident, you'll go for a slow, cheeky chip down the middle, over the diving goalkeeper?*

In modern football, we call that last one a 'Panenka', but have you ever wondered why?

Does the word mean 'cheeky chip' in one of the world's 7,000-plus languages? No.

Does it stand for:

**P**enalty?

**A**ct

**N**atural,

**E**njoy!

**N**ow

**K**ick

**A**ccurately?

No, it's not that either.

Instead, Panenka is the name of the football pioneer who first dared to take such a risky penalty, and in a really massive match: the final of Euro 1976.

Back then, the UEFA European Championship was still a pretty new tournament, and a pretty small one too. Yes, forget group stages and quarter-finals – there were only four teams! Just don't expect any easy games . . .

That year, the four finalists were:

- The hosts **Yugoslavia** (a big and diverse country in Eastern Europe, which is now six separate nations: Croatia, Serbia, Montenegro, Slovenia, Macedonia, and Bosnia and Herzegovina)
- The reigning world champions **West Germany**, captained by the legendary Franz Beckenbauer
- The 1974 World Cup runners-up **the Netherlands**, captained by the famous Johan Cruyff
- And **Czechoslovakia** . . .

In 1992, Czechoslovakia was divided to form the Czech Republic and Slovakia, but in 1976, it was still one united nation with a fearsome football team. Going into the tournament, they were unbeaten in over two years and twenty-three matches, including two wins against England!

Although Czechoslovakia didn't have any superstars like Beckenbauer or Cruyff, they were a hard-working, well-organised team with lots of talented players including their attacking midfield magician **Antonín Panenka**.

As well as a creative, skilful playmaker, Panenka was

also seen as a real set-piece specialist. For his Czech club, Bohemians Prague, he took everything: corners, free-kicks, and . . . *PENALTIES!*

For years, Panenka had kept calm and usually scored from the spot, but one particularly dirty match in 1974 had forced him to think and train a little harder. When Bohemians were awarded three penalties in one game against FC Viktoria Plzeň, Panenka took them all, but he only scored one. One goal out of three? He had work to do.

As sportswriter Ben Lyttleton tells the story, 'For the next two years, after every training session, Panenka stayed behind with Bohemians' goalkeeper Zdeněk Hruška and took penalties . . . They would bet on the outcome of the penalties, sometimes with money, but often with chocolate and beer.'

So, did Panenka soon get sleepy on his winnings? Not according to the man himself.

'To start with he [Hruška] saved a lot because he was a good keeper. But then I started thinking of new ways to succeed. I lay awake at night and thought about this. I knew that goalkeepers usually choose one side, but if you kick the ball too hard, he can save it with his leg . . .'

And so, the penalty that would soon become known as 'the Panenka' was born – a SLOW cheeky chip down the middle of the goal that a diving keeper would NOT be able to save with their legs.

The next step for Panenka was testing his new spot-kick out in friendly matches. Was it successful? Yes, except for one really wet match where the keeper stayed standing up and saved it, probably because the pitch was such a mud-bath that he didn't want to dive!

Oh well, it was all good experience, and with each penalty he took, Panenka perfected his technique, until at last he was ready to use it in proper matches, for club and maybe even country . . .

First up for Czechoslovakia, in the 1976 Euro semi-finals: the Netherlands.

The Dutch were the clear favourites to win, but as the rain poured down, it was Panenka, not Cruyff, who created the first goal of the game. In the 19th minute, he set up Ondruš with one of his fantastic free-kicks. *1–0!*

Wow, Czechoslovakia were winning, and it stayed that way until midway through the second half when first their midfielder Jaroslav Pollák was sent off, and then Ondruš scored again with a brilliant volley, but at the wrong end this time. *1–1!*

And that was still the scoreline after 90 minutes when the referee blew the final whistle. Time for extra-time . . . and penalties? No, not on this occasion because Czechoslovakia managed to score two very late match-winners – in the 114th and 118th minutes!

Against the odds, Czechoslovakia were through to the Euro '76 final, where they faced the World Champions, West Germany.

Ooof, it was all set to be a real battle at the Red Star Stadium in Belgrade. But after 25 frantic minutes, Czechoslovakia were already 2–0 up, thanks to goals from Švehlík and Karol Dobiaš. Woah, what a start! Now, could they hold on for a famous victory? Not quite, Dieter Müller pulled one goal back before half-time, and then Bernd Hölzenbein equalised for Germany in the very last minute. *2–2!*

Nooooooooooo!

Oh well, it wasn't over yet for Czechoslovakia. There was still extra-time, and then . . . PENALTIES!

It was the first time a Euro final had ever been decided by a shoot-out, and do you want to hear something totally shocking? In the build-up to the tournament, West Germany hadn't even practised penalties! There were two main reasons for that:

1. As Euro and World Champions, they were being a bit arrogant (probably).

2. The shoot-out wasn't actually agreed until a few hours before kick-off! In the past, Euro finals had gone to replays, but in 1976, the Germans asked UEFA for penalties instead because their team was too tired for a second match.

*A penalty shoot-out? Oh OK!* The Germany players only found out the plan during the warm-up, when it was too late for them to even practise. Czechoslovakia, on the other hand, were fully prepared. In fact, their manager Václav Ježek had even organised a shoot-out in proper match conditions, at the end of a friendly, in front of 10,000 fans!

So, it was no surprise when winger Marián Masný, Zdeněk Nehoda and captain Anton Ondruš all stepped up and scored for Czechoslovakia.

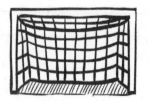

But despite their lack of training, so did the first three takers for Germany.

*3–3*

Eventually someone had to miss, but who would it be?

Ladislav Jurkemik for Czechoslovakia? No, he blasted the ball into the net.

Uli Hoeneß for Germany? Yes, he blasted the ball high over the bar!

Czechoslovakia were now just one successful spot-kick away from becoming European Champions, and who was walking forward to take it? Yep, Panenka!

'Antonin, please don't try one of your cheeky chips – not now!' his manager pleaded, but did Panenka listen? No, of course he didn't!

**'I wanted to give the fans something new to see, to create something that would get them talking . . . I wanted football to be more than just kicking a ball.'**

But what if Panenka's spot-kick was saved? He would look silly for trying something so risky! Yet if he scored, this would be his big moment, his chance to make football history . . .

He began with a long run-up, so that he could study the German keeper carefully. *What would Sepp Maier do?* The answer was: 'dive to the left'. Perfect! So, with a skilful jab of his right foot, Panenka chipped a shot slowly and cheekily down the middle.

The ball sailed beautifully through the air, then dropped down into the back of the net.

What a way to win the Euros for his country – with a

piece of pure football ART! Panenka threw both arms up in the air and raced away to enjoy his magical, ground-breaking moment.

Panenka himself retired from international football after the 1982 World Cup, but his classic penalty? Oh, that lives on and on and on . . .

- *Zinedine Zidane, France vs Italy – 2006 World Cup final*
- *Andrea Pirlo, Italy vs England – Euro 2016 quarter-finals*
- *Karim Benzema, Real Madrid vs Manchester City, 2022 Champions League semi-finals*
- *Achraf Hakimi, Morocco vs Spain, 2022 World Cup, Round of 16 . . .*

But don't worry, Antonin – no matter how many players try, your original 'Panenka' will never, ever be beaten.

## Three Cheers for the Two-Footed Footballers!

'Don't forget to practise with your weaker foot!'

If you're a keen young footballer, I bet you've heard phrases like that before (somewhere between one and ten thousand times). So, what do you think – wise words or a waste of time?

Being able to play with both feet might not seem like the most useful football superpower (I mean, imagine if you could fly!), but as this last unbelievable story shows, you never know when you might need it to save the day . . .

Let me set the scene for you – after 120 minutes of tense, tiring football in boiling-hot sunshine, the 1999 FIFA Women's World Cup final between the USA, the tournament hosts, and China has ended in . . . a 0–0 draw.

*Wow, call that entertainment?!*

Look, I'm sure the ninety thousand fans watching live

253

at the Rose Bowl in California would have liked to see at least one goal scored, but hey, there was hopefully still more exciting drama to come. Because what comes after extra-time? That's right . . . PENALTIES!

After a short break for both teams to pick their takers and drink lots of ice-cold water, the spot-kicks began:

*China substitute Xie Huilin . . . GOAL!*

*USA captain Carla Overbeck . . . GOAL!*

*Qiu Haiyan . . . GOAL!*

*Joy Fawcett . . . GOAL!*

Hmmm maybe this shoot-out was going to go on as long as the actual game!

But no, when Liu Ying stepped up next, Briana Scurry sprang forward and made a diving save.

*Advantage USA!* Now, they just needed to keep scoring, which Kristine Lilly and Mia Hamm both did. The USA were nearly there now; they just needed to score their last penalty, and they would be crowned World Champions for the second time!

So, who had manager Tony DiCicco chosen to take

that potentially World Cup-winning spot-kick?

No, not forward Shannon MacMillan.

No, not midfielder Tisha Venturini either.

At the last minute, the USA coach had changed the order, bumping up his left-back, **Brandi Chastain**, from sixth to fifth.

Wait a second – *the left-back?* Yes, but don't be fooled by her position; Chastain was originally a forward, not a defender. After losing her place in the USA squad for the 1995 World Cup, however, she had decided to turn herself into a different kind of player, the kind of player that her country needed most: a speedy, hard-working left-back!

For a while, Chastain had also been the USA's main penalty taker, but a few months earlier, Michelle Akers had taken over, after Chastain hit the crossbar in a match against . . . yep, you guessed it – China! Now, she was up against the same team and the same keeper, Gao Hong, again. So, was Chastain going to do anything differently this time? Oh yes, she was about to do something that China's keeper would certainly not be expecting . . .

You see, in the team huddle before penalties, DiCicco had spoken to Chastain and said something that would strike fear into the heart of any footballer:

*'I want you to take it with your other foot.'*

Now, I know what you're probably thinking right now: *WHAT?! WHY?! No way, don't do it, Brandi – this is THE WORLD CUP FINAL!*

Do you know what Chastain said, though? *'Sure, Coach'.* Or something like that, anyway . . .

But before you get too carried away thinking these people have completely lost their minds, there are a couple of pretty major things I should mention:

1. While Chastain was naturally right-footed, she had always played football with both feet. It was something that her father had taught her as a young girl growing up in California, and she'd practised for hours, kicking a ball against a wall again and again until her left foot was just as

good as her right. It was why she made a good left-back, and a good left-footed penalty taker too . . .

2. Her coach's request didn't catch Chastain by surprise; she had been practising left-footed penalties for a while, and with great success. Her right-foot strikes had become too predictable, always going to the same side of the goal. 'It got to the point that goalkeepers knew where she would kick,' DiCicco explains. Her miss against China? Right foot! But when she switched to using her left, Chastain found that her shooting was even more accurate, and it was also more difficult to guess where the ball would go. Much better!

OK, now back to the big shoot-out and Chastain on her long walk forward from the halfway line . . .

For a lot of people, the idea of taking a high-pressure penalty in front of ninety thousand fans would be more of a nightmare than a dream come true, but not for

Chastain. In fact, that was the third, and maybe most important, reason why DiCicco had picked her to take the USA's fifth and final spot-kick:

1. She was good at penalties
2. She could kick with her left foot
**3. She was the ultimate big-game player!**

Yes, Chastain was one of the strongest characters in the women's game.

This was a player who had suffered the disappointment of missing the 1995 World Cup, but then bounced back to master a completely different position for her country.

This was a player who had also scored a horror own-goal in the 1999 quarter-finals against Germany, but then bounced back to score an equalising goal later in the same game!

This was a player who loved being the centre of attention so much that her teammates called her 'Hollywood'!

**'BRANDI WANTS TO HAVE THE RESPONSIBILITY ON HER. SOME PLAYERS ARE AFRAID OF FAILURE, THEY DON'T WANT THE ROLE. BRANDI WANTS IT. SHE WANTS THE SPOTLIGHT. THAT'S THE TYPE OF PLAYER YOU WANT IN PENALTY KICKS.'**

– USA coach Tony DiCicco

So instead of nerves and doubts, Chastain was full of confidence. 'When I walked up, I was like, "This is going in. We're going to be Champions."'

Go, Brandi! During their last penalty battle, Gao had put her off by walking along her line and winking and smiling, but this time, Chastain didn't even look up. There was no need; she knew where she was going to place the ball – just inside the right post, with as much power as possible . . . and with her left foot!

Chastain didn't want to spoil the big surprise, though, so as she waited for the referee's whistle, she stood in the centre, keeping the keeper guessing . . .

*FWEET!! . . . . . . BANG!*

**'It was like a complete slow-motion between my foot and the net . . . It seemed to take forever and as it travelled, everything was so quiet and still and slow. And when it hit the net: an explosion! Noise, cheering, cameras, teammates, everything.'**

*. . . GOAL!*

Yes, Chastain had done it; with her 'weaker' left foot, she had scored the perfect penalty. She was the USA's World Cup-winning hero! In a moment of pure joy, she took off her shirt and waved it in the air, before falling to her knees and punching the air with both fists.

Sound familiar, Lionesses fans? Yes, that celebration has become so iconic in women's football that twenty-three years later, England star Chloe Kelly decided to recreate it after scoring an extra-time winner against Germany in the UEFA Women's Euro 2022 final.

But don't worry, Brandi, you'll always be the first, the original, and besides, Kelly scored with her stronger right foot, and from two yards, rather than twelve!

# The Goalie with the Magic Gloves

If your football team really wanted to win a penalty shoot-out, which keeper would you call?

Emi Martínez?
Mary Earps?
Simon Bloch Jorgensen, the world's tallest-ever keeper? (He's 2.1 m in case you wondered!)

No, the stopper you need is Nahuel Guzmán.

Who?

You might not have heard of him but trust me – he's the goalie with the magic gloves!

Guzmán won six caps for his country, Argentina, between 2014 and 2017, but it's at club level that he has worked most of his many wonders. In 2014, he moved to the Mexican team Club de Fútbol Tigres de la Universidad Autónoma de Nuevo León . . . or 'Tigres' for short. There, he set to work, winning shoot-outs with his special powers . . .

In 2015, Tigres were crowned Champions of Mexico after beating Pumas on penalties, and who was their hero? Yes, Guzmán!

Starting in a strange low, crouching position, he sprang up like a frog to save the crucial spot-kick.

A year later, Guzmán did it again, only this time his performance was even more magical. In the shoot-out against América, he somehow saved ALL three penalties: low to his left, then straight down the middle, then high to his right – amazing!

As word spread about the wizard in the Tigres goal, penalty takers started working harder to beat him, and so Guzmán had to find new weird and wonderful ways to win the battle.

In the 2023 Leagues Cup, Tigres' Round of 32 clash against the Vancouver Whitecaps went all the way to penalties. No problem, Guzmán had been practising and he had some exciting new tricks to try out . . .

As the second Whitecaps player stepped up, Guzmán moved along his goal-line patting the air with his gloves and . . . pretending to be trapped inside a box!

*What?! Why?!*

Well, alongside his love of football, the keeper also had other passions that he wanted to express and explore on the pitch. 'I come from an artistic family,' he explained after the game. 'I have friends who for many years have worked as clowns. It's part of their lifestyle. They're like my advisors.'

Riiiiiiight! It was certainly an entertaining moment, but would the mime act work? No, Sergio Córdova still scored.

Guzmán didn't do anything unusual for the next spot-kick, but as the fourth player stepped up, the Tigres keeper decided it was time for something bigger and better. When he suddenly turned around in his goal, holding his nose, the fans thought something was wrong. That's when he started pulling a really, really long piece of multi-coloured paper out of his mouth!

*WHAT?!*

The referee wasn't impressed – yellow card!

Oh well, more importantly, would Guzmán's weird trick work?

Yes!

It's hard to say whether Ranko Veselinović was mesmerised by the magic, just tired, or just terrible at penalties, but he didn't put much power on his shot and the Tigres keeper dived down to make the save.

Hurrraaaaaay, Guzmán was their spot-kick hero once again!

In the next round, Tigres were drawing 0–0 when their opponents Monterrey were awarded a last-minute penalty. Ooooooooh, what would Guzmán do next? This time, he leaned forward on his goal-line and wobbled his legs, as if he was trying to balance on a wire, high up in the sky! *WHAT?!*

So, did the trapeze act work? No, sadly for Tigres, Sergio Canales stayed focused and scored, but hey, the keeper magic was fun while it lasted.

## Conclusion

*That's it, folks – book over, and what a rollercoaster of football emotions it's been! Over the last 120 (plus eight) minutes, we've really had it all:*

*Incredible comebacks*

*Funny fails*

*Embarrassing moments*

*Shocking red cards*

*Last-minute match-winners*

*High-pressure penalties*

***and so much more.***

*I mean, come on – who could ever get bored of this beautiful game?!*

*So, shake hands, swap shirts, and join us again next time for more . . . **UNBELIEVABLE FOOTBALL!***

# ACKNOWLEDGEMENTS

Wow, we did it – *Unbelievable Football* 5! Like wave after wave of Manchester City attacks, the incredible true football stories just keep coming. This book was an absolutely joy to research and write, and hopefully, it'll be a joy to read too. I'd like to say a massive thank you to:

**My editorial dream team:** Victoria Walsh, Davina Rungasamy, Adele Brimacombe and Laura 'The Gaffer' Horsley

**Illustrator extraordinaire:** Ollie Mann

**Director of football:** Nick Walters

**Assistant managers:** Iona, Arlo and Lila

**Team mascot:** Claude the Sausage Dog

And most important of all:

**The supporters:** family, friends, authors, teachers, booksellers, librarians, and of course, readers. This book, like football itself, would be nothing without the fans.

# SOURCES

**The Horse Who Saved the FA Cup Final**
Whitehead, Richard. *The Cup* (Pitch Publishing, 2022).
*Encyclopedia of British Football* (Psychology Press, 2002).
'#50GreatestMatches - #46 Bolton Wanderers 2-0 West Ham United.' West Ham United Football Club, 15 May 2020. https://tinyurl.com/t98m4f34, accessed 19 May 2024.

**The Doctor Who Played His Part on the Pitch**
Muamba, Fabrice. *I'm Still Standing* (Trinity Mirror Sport Media, 2012).
Taylor, Daniel. 'Muamba reunited with doctors who saved him.' The Athletic, 15 March 2022. https://tinyurl.com/2s46k85r, accessed 19 March 2024.

**The Filipinas Who Wowed the Women's Football World**
Nazareno, Mia. 'Squad Goals: Making History With the Filipinas Football Team.' *Vogue*, 30 September 2023. https://tinyurl.com/2c2fkmhv, accessed 19 March 2024.

**WEIRD & WONDERFUL The Two Watches of Diego Maradona**
Bendictus, Luke. 'Hublot CEO explains why Diego Maradona wore two watches.' Time and Tide, 22 April 2022. https://tinyurl.com/f82mfs7h, accessed 19 March 2024.

**The 'One-Handed God' Who Won the World Cup**
'El Divino Manco: The one-armed World Cup winner.' A Halftime Report, 26 February 2016. https://tinyurl.com/2vhuprh3, accessed 19 March 2024.

**The Red Dragons Who Came Roaring Back (With a Little Help from Hollywood!)**
Herbert, Ian. *Tinseltown* (Headline, 2023).
'"Unlike anything I've ever seen before!" Incredible Ryan Reynolds interview after Wrexham go clear.' TNT Sports, YouTube, 10 April 2023. https://tinyurl.com/2ntfsj9y, accessed 19 March 2024.

**The Remarkable Return of Mary Queen of Stops**
Ward, Tom. 'Mary Earps's big save.' *GQ*, 3 July 2023. https://tinyurl.com/3zadt5xm, accessed 19 March 2024.
Geall, Megan. 'Mary Earps almost quit professional football – until Sarina Wiegman

gave her a chance.' *Women's Health*, 20 July 2023. https://tinyurl.com/2dwh7yy9, accessed 19 March 2024.

**A Christmas Day to Forget for the Seagulls**

'I'll never forget the day Albion lost 18–0.' The Argus, 3 December 2001. https://tinyurl.com/4ad5re6u, accessed 19 March 2024.

**Nice One, Sonny – Hero for Club AND Country**

Pearce, Ben. 'Son Heung-Min sorry for leaving Tottenham to play in Asian Games.' ESPN, 31 July 2018. https://tinyurl.com/mvzff4wp, accessed 19 March 2024.

Johnson, Greg. 'Why Son Heung-min is thankful to Spurs over Asian Games win amid military service rumours.' Football.London, 2 September 2018. https://tinyurl.com/36hb8m5z, accessed 19 March 2024.

'Tottenham's Son Heung-min says he enjoyed his "tough" military service.' *Guardian*, 3 June 2020. https://tinyurl.com/3xrf4vxk, accessed 19 March 2024.

**The Four Keepers of Comoros**

Dove, Ed. 'COVID-19: AFCON debutants Comoros forced to use outfield player as goalkeeper.' 23 January 2022. https://tinyurl.com/34mvjda5, accessed 19 March 2024.

**WEIRD & WONDERFUL: The Battle of Bramall Lane**

'Battle of Bramall Lane abandoned.' BBC News, 16 March 2002. https://tinyurl.com/3vsxhfvv, accessed 19 March 2024.

Hall, Danny. '"I'm not sure I'd do anything differently . . ." – Patrick Suffo remembers Sheffield United's infamous "Battle of Bramall Lane" with West Brom, 18 years on.' The Star, 21 March 2020. https://tinyurl.com/yc6meyba, accessed 19 March 2024.

**The Clever Couple Who Came Up with Yellow and Red Cards**

'Battle of Santiago.' YouTube, 14 December 2007. https://tinyurl.com/2fuewfwb, accessed 19 March 2024.

Stamp, Jimmy, 'Who invented the Yellow Card?' *Smithsonian Magazine*, 8 July 2014. https://tinyurl.com/yc4aa5tc, accessed 19 March 2024.

**Cheating Chile and How Not to Beat a Team Like Brazil**

Edwards, Piers. 'World Cup scandal! The unbelievable plot to eliminate Brazil.' CNN, 18 June 2014. https://tinyurl.com/236rsm65, accessed 19 March 2024.

**Zizou Loses His Head**

Spiro, Matthew. *Sacré Bleu* (Biteback Publishing, 2020).

Adamson, Mike. 'Zidane apologises for headbutt.' *Guardian*, 12 July 2006. https://tinyurl.com/4ekfhfsa, accessed 19 March 2024.

**Football 3 Hitler 0**
Correia, Mickaël. *A People's History of Football* (Pluto Press, 2023).

**The Footballer Who Stole *The Scream***
*The Man Who Stole* The Scream. Apple TV, 2023.

**Meet . . . the Ultimate Football Mega-Fans!**
Butler, Josh. 'The football fan who has collected 3,000 shirts from around the world.' *Guardian*, 2 February 2022. https://tinyurl.com/rjxa2jxr, accessed 19 March 2024.

Sanchez, Luisa. 'Mexican football fan collects 1,230 different balls to break record.' Guinness World Records, 24 November 2021. https://tinyurl.com/38jpj7yc, accessed 19 March 2024.

'Nobody compares to Maria Petri.' *Mundial*. https://tinyurl.com/36xk3n7u, accessed 19 March 2024.

**The Lancashire Lads Who Taught the 'Old Boys' a Football Lesson**
Whitehead, Richard. *The Cup* (Pitch Publishing, 2022).

Pope, Conor. 'Why the real history behind the English Game matters – and what it tells us about modern football.' FourFourTwo, 10 April 2020. https://tinyurl.com/4ehset77, accessed 19 March 2024.

'Blackburn Olympic vs Old Etonians 2–1 (English FA Cup Final: March 31, 1883).' Play Up, Liverpool. https://tinyurl.com/5dhmd3pa, accessed 19 March 2024.

**The Lancashire Lasses Who Kept Calm and Carried On Playing**
Williams, Jean. *The History of Women's Football* (Pen & Sword History, 2011).

**The Rise and Fall – and Rise Again – of Brazil's Brilliant Black Footballers**
Bellos, Alex. *Futebol* (Bloomsbury Paperbacks, 2014).

Correia, Mickaël. *A People's History of Football* (Pluto Press, 2023).

**WEIRD & WONDERFUL: Get Ready for . . . the RoboCup!**
RoboCup. https://tinyurl.com/yvhrxv4k, accessed 19 March 2024.

**From Kenya to Qatar: The Humble Hero Who Sent the Socceroos to the World Cup**
'Australia's Awer Mabil: "Football has been my life's guide".' *Guardian*, 21 November 2022. https://tinyurl.com/yc2w4awh, accessed 19 March 2024.

Keane, Daniel. 'Awer Mabil's journey from refugee camp to the World Cup is the stuff that dreams are made of.' ABC News, 15 June 2022. https://tinyurl.com/5fdjhxtj, accessed 19 March 2024.

'Awer Mabil: Sudanese refugee says his penalty is "a thank you to Australia".' BBC Sport, 14 June 2022. https://tinyurl.com/2p9n73xh, accessed 19 March 2024.

'Awer Mabil used to make footballs from plastic bags. Now he's an Australian hero.'

SBS News. https://tinyurl.com/kp9nb3da, accessed 19 March 2024.

**Las 15 Who Fought for a Better Football World and Won**

Cervelló Herrero, Laia. 'This Barca-Madrid rivalry is getting intense — the dispute driving it remains unsolved.' The Athletic, 20 January 2023. https://tinyurl.com/4rxfr3nj, accessed 19 March 2024.

Kirby, Paul. 'Spain's Hermoso says image tarnished by Rubiales World Cup kiss.' BBC News. https://tinyurl.com/4che9p7a, accessed 19 March 2024.

Wrack, Suzanne. 'Spain's World Cup-winning squad to continue boycott of national team.' _Guardian_, 15 September 2023. https://tinyurl.com/55padsk3, accessed 19 March 2024.

Lev, Jacob. 'Spanish soccer players speak out on "systemic discrimination" ahead of first match since Women's World Cup win.' CNN, 22 September 2023. https://tinyurl.com/y5v9y5we, accessed 19 March 2024.

**The Midfielder with Extra Motivation to Run**

'Marshall Munetsi: "I will continue to use my voice to help the next generation".' FIFPRO, 28 March 2023. https://tinyurl.com/3wtv5jju, accessed 19 March 2024.

'Marshall Munetsi: "The more I run, the more we raise for underprivileged children in Zimbabwe".' FIFPRO, 6 June 2023. https://tinyurl.com/yc4xxr3e, accessed 19 March 2024.

Marshall Munetsi Foundation. https://tinyurl.com/2mmtxuny, accessed 19 March 2024.

**The Incredible Injury-Time Adventures of Džeko, Balotelli and Agüeroooooooooooooooooooo!**

Agüero, Sergio. _Born to Rise_ (Trinity Mirror Sport Media, 2015).

Clayton, David. 'Aguero: "I told them to leave me alone!".' Manchester City, 19 June 2022. https://tinyurl.com/5n6mzcx2, accessed 19 March 2024.

**A Cheeky Chip that Changed Penalties Forever**

Lyttleton, Ben. _Twelve Yards_ (Bantam Press, 2014).

**WEIRD & WONDERFUL: The Goalie with the Magic Gloves**

Cardenas, Felipe. 'Tigres' Nahuel Guzman on his goal-line magic trick, Messi, and taking influence from clowns.' The Athletic, 25 August 2023. https://tinyurl.com/3e9db484, accessed 19 March 2024.

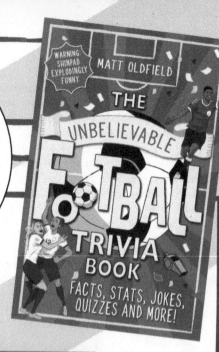

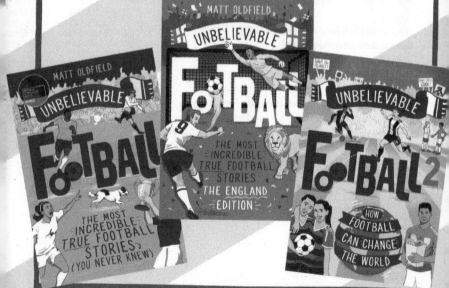